BMW 3 Series

The Complete Story

Other Titles in the Crowood AutoClassics Series

BMW 3 Series
The Complete Story

James Taylor

First published in 2000 by
The Crowood Press Ltd
Ramsbury, Marlborough
Wiltshire SN8 2HR

British Library Cataloguing-in-Publication Data
A catalogue record for this book is available from the
British Library.

ISBN 1 86126 317 1

Acknowledgements
The author is grateful to the following: *BMW Car* magazine,
BMW Mobile Tradition, BMW (GB) and Steve Warner.

Typeset by Florence Production Ltd, Stoodleigh, Devon
Printed and bound in Great Britain by The Bath Press

Contents

Evolution

Modern BMWs – and that includes all of the 3 Series ranges – have a factory type code beginning with E. This E probably stands for *Entwurf* ('design') and is allocated at the design stage; the numerical order therefore relates to the date when design commenced, and not to the date when a model entered production. Not every project has made it past the design stage, and there are therefore many gaps in the sequence of numbers associated with the production BMWs.

The first E series codes were allocated in the mid-sixties. What follows is a list of the main production models since then, with the 3 Series cars highlighted in bold type.

E3   2500, 2800 and subsequent big saloons of this range, 1968–77
E6   Facelifted '02 models, 1973–75 (The original '02s did not have an E code)
E9   Six-cylinder coupés from 2500CS to 3.0CSL, 1968–71
E10   2002 turbo, variant of the E6 '02 models, 1973–75
E12   First-generation 5 Series saloons, 1972–81
E21   First-generation 3 Series, 1975–82
E23   First-generation 7 Series saloons, 1977–86
E24   6 Series coupés, 1976–89
E26   M1 mid-engined supercar, 1978–80
E28   Second-generation 5 Series, 1981–88
E30   Second-generation 3 Series, 1983–91
E31   8 Series coupés, 1989 on
E32   Second-generation 7 Series, 1986–94
E34   Third-generation 5 Series saloons, 1988–96
E36   Third-generation 3 Series, 1991 on
E38   Third-generation 7 Series, 1994 on
E39   Fourth generation 5 Series saloons, 1995 on
E46   Fourth-generation 3 Series, 1997 on
E53   X5 sport-activity vehicle, 1999 on

1 Pedigree – BMW Before the 3 Series

When BMW launched its fourth range of cars to bear the 3 Series name in 1997, the company made much of the heritage that lay behind them. Publicity material argued that these were in fact the fifth generation of the compact BMW sports saloon, the first examples having been the 1602 of 1966 and the 2002 of 1968.

While that view perhaps complicates the issue unnecessarily in the interests of good publicity, there is little doubt about BMW's underlying claim to have invented the compact sports saloon in the 1960s. There was simply nothing else like the 1602 available in the middle of that decade, and when the 2002 was launched a couple of years later with a powerful 2-ltr engine under its bonnet, it took the motoring world by storm. The first of the cars called 3 Series models were replacements for the 1602 and 2002, and so the lineage has carried on.

However, today's 3 Series BMWs have a far more important position in the motoring scene than did those earlier saloons of the

BMW publicity viewed the pedigree of the 1998 E46 model as going back beyond the first 3 Series to the '02 models of the 1960s. Seen here, from left to right, are the '02, E21 first-generation 3 Series, E46 fourth-generation 3 Series, E30 second-generation 3 Series and E36 third-generation 3 Series.

With the introduction of coupé versions of the E36 in 1992, BMW traced the lineage even further back, to the rear-engined 700 of the early 1960s. Behind the E36 in the foreground are (left to right) a 700, an '02, an E21 first-generation 3 Series and an E30 second-generation model.

1960s. The latter were simply quick, two-door saloons with cramped interiors and a sporting demeanour. Today's BMW 3 Series range embraces family saloons with four doors, family estates, competitors to the 'hot hatches' of a class below, delicious convertibles and pocket supercar saloons. Throughout the range, it is possible to order luxury and convenience equipment that was simply unthinkable in the days of the '02 models, or even of the first-generation 3 Series.

The 3 Series has come a long way and represented a lot of cars, and with each generation of the car BMW has improved its worldwide sales. The first-generation (E21) models were built to the tune of 1,364,038 units between 1975 and 1982. The second-generation (E30) cars were even more successful, BMW selling 2,220,225 examples between 1982 and 1990. The third-generation (E36) range was introduced in 1990 and had beaten that total by December 1997 with a figure of almost 2.5 million. That, however, was far from the end, because the range was destined to stay in production for several more years as its low-volume derivatives remained available alongside the high-volume versions of the fourth-generation (E46) range, introduced in 1998.

Quite apart from finding homes with millions of owners all over the world, the 3

Series has had a profound effect on the world's motor industry. In the days of the 1602 and 2002, Triumph in Britain was among the manufacturers to see the potential in what BMW was doing, and the Dolomite Sprint of 1973 was a direct answer to the bigger-engined BMW, and with the added convenience of four doors. But one of the biggest boosts to the success of the 3 Series came while the cars were still under development, in the shape of the 1973–74 Oil Crisis. As the price of crude oil, and therefore petrol, shot up, fuel economy suddenly became a top priority for all buyers. Those who wanted sporting cars wanted machines that were just as fast as before, but also smaller and lighter. The conditions were exactly right for a car with

the pretensions of the original 3 Series, launched into the aftermath of the Oil Crisis in 1975.

BMW was fortunate: no other manufacturer was quite as well prepared for the market conditions of the later 1970s, and so the 3 Series sold strongly and developed an enviable reputation. Spotting this new market, other makers began to develop similar cars, the most significant of these being perhaps the Mercedes-Benz 190 or W201 series, which was announced in 1982. There was no doubt that it was a Mercedes interpretation of the 3 Series, with the more conservative and typically Mercedes feature of four doors instead of two. This in turn inspired Audi to get in on the act, and its current A4 is aimed directly at the 3 Series market. When Saab

BMW's sporting traditions reached right back into the 1930s, when cars like this 315/1 or 319/1 roadster made their mark on road racing.

The most successful sports car of the 1930s was the BMW 328, seen here with a special coupé body designed by Touring of Milan for the 1940 Mille Miglia.

introduced a 3 Series competitor in the 1990s, the company made no secret of what it was doing. The car was called the Saab 9-3, that second number staking its claim in the class established by the 3 Series BMW.

So the 3 Series has been enormously important in the history of motoring in the quarter-century of its existence. It capitalized on the work done by its 1602 and 2002 predecessors in opening up a new class of car, and it set the standard against which other makers' products were invariably judged. The 3 Series has become a benchmark; it has also successfully maintained the balancing act between hugely popular everyday consumer product and aspirational indulgence. It has done immeasuable

good for the BMW image wherever it has been sold, and it has helped turn BMW into one of the world's most successful car companies today. Yet BMW was by no means always so well-respected.

THE BAROQUE ANGELS

Only a decade and a half before the first 3 Series was introduced, BMW had been in very bad shape indeed. The problem was that the company had never really found its niche in the car market after the end of the Second World War in 1945. Initially, it struggled to survive in the harsh post-war economic climate, having lost its main factories: they were situated in the Soviet-occupied sector of Germany. Motorcycle production started hesitantly in 1948 and several prototype cars were built in the late forties, but it was 1951 before the company was prepared to show a new car in public, and 1952 before that car – the 501 – entered volume production.

These big, sturdy middle-class machines were the mainstay of the company's car division from 1951 to 1964. Unfortunately, they harked back too much to BMW's successful designs of the thirties, with the result that their styling dated very quickly and the cars earned the appropriate but rather disdainful nickname of *Barockengeln* – 'Baroque Angels' – because their bulbous and flowing lines reminded people of the carved wooden figures in south German and Austrian churches of the Baroque period (seventeenth and early eighteenth centuries).

The 501 started off with a revival of the much-copied pre-war 2ltr six-cylinder engine, but it was a heavy and cumbersome machine and not even a succession of 2.6ltr and 3.2ltr V8 engines could turn it into a really credible contender in the marketplace. Attempts to find export sales in the USA with sports and grand touring models based on the Baroque Angels' running-gear were none too successful, either.

The first 501s had an updated version of the pre-war 2ltr six-cylinder engine. In 1954 this was supplemented by a 2.6ltr V8 with around 50 per cent more power; the six-cylinder 501 was also uprated, and coupé and cabriolet bodies were announced.

In 1955, BMW announced the 502 range, basically the same cars with extra equipment. These had either an uprated 2.6ltr V8 or a new big-bore 3.2ltr V8. The 501 V8 remained unchanged, but the six-cylinder

Even the attractive convertible coachwork cannot hide the fact that this 502 from the mid-1950s was actually a large and rather cumbersome car.

501s were given an enlarged 2.1ltr engine. Then the 3.2ltr V8 was in turn uprated for 1957's 502 3.2ltr Super. In 1958, the 502 models were renamed as the BMW 2.6ltr, BMW 3.2ltr and BMW 3.2ltr Super. 501 V8 production ended, but the six-cylinder 501s remained available with their original names.

Front disc brakes and the (formerly optional) servo became standard on the 3.2

The 503

The 503 was one way in which BMW hoped to crack the American market in the mid-fifties. The Baroque Angel saloons were not going to sell well in the USA, but BMW thought that an elegant grand tourer with the saloon's running gear and powerful V8 engine might.

The 503 used the saloon's perimeter-frame chassis as well as its running gear, and it had an all-alloy body designed by Albrecht Goertz. Goertz was a German who had worked with the Raymond Loewy design studio on Studebakers in the late forties and early fifties, then became a naturalized American and set up his own design studio. He was persuaded to submit designs for the 503 (and the 507) by BMW's American importer, Max Hoffmann. Tempted by Hoffmann's offer to take a Goertz-designed 503 in quantity, BMW embraced the Goertz proposals and showed a prototype at the 1955 Frankfurt Show. Production began the following May.

Sadly, the 503's styling was flawed. The long bonnet hinted at power, but was spoiled by an ugly snub nose incorporating the traditional BMW grille. Electric windows were advanced for the time, and the power-operated hood on the cabriolets was a first for a German car. But the saloon gearbox, mounted remotely from the engine and operated by a woolly column change, did the 503 no favours. After September 1957, the gearbox was mounted conventionally so that a floor change could be fitted.

The 503 was always an expensive and exclusive car, competing with such exotics as the (more costly) Mercedes-Benz 300Sc and the Bentley Continental. Production averaged 100 or so a year, and it is likely that no two examples were exactly alike. Only a handful were delivered with right-hand drive. Despite their aesthetic shortcomings, these cars are very much sought-after today.

BMW tried to break into the market for exotic machinery in the USA with this 503 cabriolet, but the company's gamble did not pay off.

Super in 1959 and on the ordinary 3.2 a year later. Then in 1961, the six-cylinder 501s ceased production. The 2.6ltr was renamed the 2600, given the servo and front discs, and joined by a 2600L with more power and better trim. The 3.2 became a 3200L and the 3.2 Super became a 3200 Super (also known as a 3200S). Its 160bhp V8 made it the fastest saloon then made in Germany and among the fastest in the world.

The last of 21,807 Baroque Angels were built in March 1964.

THE ISETTA

With these cars, BMW was aiming at a fairly wealthy clientele who wanted large and powerful cars, and inevitably the cost of these cars limited their sales success. To counterbalance this and achieve volume sales, the company decided to go ahead with a licence-built version of the Italian Isetta 'bubble-car' in 1955.

BMW built the Isetta under licence from Iso S.p.a., who were primarily makers of motor scooters and three-wheeler utility vehicles. Iso introduced the Isetta in 1953, and also sold a licence for its production to Velam in France. Iso's owner, Count Renzo Rivolta, eventually spent the profits from these agreements on making the Euro-American Iso-Rivolta and Iso Grifo supercars.

The BMW Isetta 250 dispensed with Iso's two-stroke engine, using instead the four-stroke 247cc single-cylinder from the R25 motorcycle. From February 1956, there was a companion-model Isetta 300, with the more powerful 297cc engine from the R27 motorcycle. Other changes included smaller headlamp cowls after 1955 and a completely revised glass area with larger side windows from October 1956.

The original Iso car, the BMW version and the Velam all had twin rear wheels, but a version of the Isetta 300 built under licence from BMW in Britain from 1958 actually had a single rear wheel, because three-wheelers attracted less Purchase Tax and their road fund licence was cheaper! Just 1,750 three-wheelers were built.

In the mid-fifties, the Isetta cost just 20 per cent as much as the cheapest of the Baroque Angel 501 saloons. It sold quite well, and went on to inspire the larger, improved BMW 600 four-wheeler, but its sales were not enough to offset the losses sustained when motorcycle sales nose-dived in the mid-fifties.

THE 600

The 600 was a logical progression from the Isetta that must have seemed like a good idea at the time, but sales of just over 34,000 in two years never really matched BMW's expectations. Part of the problem was the price: the 600 was only barely cheaper than the entry-level VW Beetle. But it was also undeniable that buyers in the late fifties wanted cars that looked like cars, and were losing interest in economy models which suggested that their owners might not have much money. Without the short-lived vogue for economy cars which followed the Suez crisis of 1956–57 and its accompanying petrol shortages, the 600 might have flopped badly.

Designed by Willy Black, the 600 was unashamedly intended as an enlarged Isetta with more power and a 'proper' four-wheel configuration. Its front end was pretty much unchanged from the Isetta's, but the wheelbase had been stretched to accommodate four seats, and a conventional rear axle had been added. This introduced to BMW the semi-trailing-arm independent suspension which would be seen on almost every new model for the next four decades.

The extra size and weight demanded a more powerful engine than the Isetta's, and so the 600 had yet another motorcycle powerplant – this time the 582cc twin from BMW's recently-defunct R67. Top speed was 64mph.

THE 507

The 507 is probably the most widely-recognized classic BMW of the Fifties. Like its great rival, the Mercedes-Benz 300SL, it was inspired by the US importer Max Hoffmann, who told BMW he could sell a high-performance sports car in large quantities if the company could deliver.

In 1954, Ernst Loof designed and built a prototype on the 502 chassis with a 2.6ltr V8 engine. However, an alternative style put forward by Albrecht Goertz at Hoffmann's suggestion won the day. The Goertz style was for a curvaceous roadster with optional hard top. It was a shape which has worn incredibly well over the years, and examples of the 507 now change hands for very large sums of money.

The production cars had the 3.2ltr V8 in twin-carburettor form with 150bhp or, for the USA only, with 165bhp. Acceleration and top speed depended on which of the three optional axle ratios was chosen, but the performance of a 507 was broadly comparable to that of the contemporary Jaguar XK140. BMW claimed a 507 was capable of 136mph (219km/h) with the tallest 3.42:1 gearing, although 120mph (193km/h) was probably nearer the truth.

Yet this remarkable machine was never a strong seller. One problem was cost; another was BMW's inability to get production under way. Despite being announced at Frankfurt in 1955, the first cars were not delivered until the next year. By then, the Mercedes had become too well-entrenched

as the definitive supercar, and the 300SL coupé's mutation into a roadster model in 1957 removed the 507's most obvious advantage. Lack of boot space in the first cars was also a major failing, and BMW was forced to introduce a smaller 'optional' fuel tank to free up more room.

Just 254 507s were sold between 1956 and 1959, all with left-hand drive. Some of the very last had disc brakes at the front instead of the all-drum system.

CRISIS AND REBIRTH

These disparate model ranges made it difficult for BMW as a car maker to present any kind of real corporate image in the fifties. On the one hand there were tiny economy cars, and on the other there were large saloons and exotic sports and grand touring cars. In between there was nothing, and that made it hard for the public to make sense of BMW. The company recognized that it needed a car range to fill that yawning gap, not least because the medium-sized saloon sector was a particularly lucrative one. However, attempts to design such a car came to naught because the company lacked the money to get it into production. Consequently, throughout the fifties there was no direct equivalent of the 5 Series cars which would later make the company's reputation.

THE 700

BMW began to claw its way back into the mainstream of the car market with a delightful new small car called the 700, introduced in 1959. The 700 was really the car which pulled BMW around in the late fifties. Once again it was an upward progression in size from what had gone before – this time, the 600 chassis was stretched.

By the time it entered production, however, the 700 had become BMW's first unitary-construction car.

The 700 was again masterminded by Willy Black, the man who had designed the 600 which it replaced. Black drew on the company's motorcycle technology once again, although this time he enlarged the twin-cylinder engine of the R67 motorcycle to get the power he needed for this larger car. Styling was by the Italian Giovanni Michelotti, and its themes certainly echoed those of his Triumph Herald, an exact contemporary of the 700. His first sketch was for a slant-roof coupé, which appealed to BMW although they wanted more room in the passenger cabin. Michelotti therefore sketched up a saloon variant – never as pretty – and the Bavarians decided to build them both. The 700 Coupé entered production in August 1959 and the 700 Saloon joined it at the end of the year.

Even though the 700 was more expensive than a VW Beetle, its chic Italian styling brought in the buyers. Over the six years of its production, the car sold more than 188,000 examples and became BMW's best-selling car since 1945.

Engine power increased over those six years, and from 1961 there was an upmarket Luxus version. Then in 1962, the 700 was renamed the BMW LS. Among the most desirable of these small cars is the Baur-built cabriolet, but the most exciting was the limited-production 700RS, a competition roadster of which just nineteen were built between 1961 and 1963.

THE NEUE KLASSE CARS

The 700 sold well, but it arrived too late to stave off a financial crisis. By the end of 1959 BMW was in a bad way, having lost 15 million Deutschmarks on a turnover of 150 million marks. A general meeting of shareholders was called during December and there was strong support for a proposal from the bank which was BMW's chief creditor that the company should sell out. The

Even the little 700 Sport was pressed into service as a competitions machine. Hans Stuck is seen at the wheel of the car which gained him the German Hillclimb championship in 1960.

most likely buyer was BMW's arch-rival, Mercedes-Benz.

However, the proposal was blocked by a substantial minority of shareholders, who voted for a counter-proposal to find another source of funding which would enable BMW to remain independent. No doubt a good deal of wheeling and dealing was done behind the scenes but, over the next two months, two businessmen who already owned a substantial proportion of BMW shares began to increase their holdings. By the autumn of 1960, some two-thirds of BMW shares belonged to the brothers Harald and Herbert Quandt, and BMW once again had funds.

There had been some work done on a medium-sized saloon during the fifties, but the whole project was scrapped after the Quandt take-over and a completely new project was initiated, led by engineering chief Fritz Fiedler. Right from the begin-

ning, it was always known as the *Neue Klasse* ('new class'), and was designed to plug the gap between the 700 and the Baroque Angel saloons, which would remain in production until 1964. The Neue Klasse was designed from the outset to be the car which BMW so desperately needed – and it proved to be right on target.

The 700 had pioneered unitary construction and semi-trailing arm rear suspension at BMW, and both features were retained for the new car. Chassis engineer Eberhard Wolff chose MacPherson strut front suspension (the car was one of the earliest to have it) with an anti-roll bar to give good handling. Styling and body engineering were entrusted to Wilhelm Hofmeister, and he established a distinctive 'BMW look' for the car, with a low waistline, large glass area, slim roof pillars, flat bonnet and boot and straight-through wing lines. On the engine side, Alex von Falkenhausen resur-

The Neue Klasse saloon of the 1960s put BMW back on the road to financial health. It also earned a formidable reputation on the racetrack, and is seen here in 1800TI/SA form with Hubert Hahne at the wheel in the 1965 Francorchamps 24-hour event.

After BMW bought Glas in 1966, some of that company's designs were rebadged as BMWs. This is the 1600GT, with BMW's own engine replacing the 1700 which Glas had previously used in the car.

rected sketches originally made in 1958 for a 1ltr ohc four-cylinder engine originally intended for the 700 range, and developed these into an oversquare 1.5ltr alloy-head masterpiece with built-in stretchability.

Though the 1500 was shown in prototype form at Frankfurt in 1961, it was nowhere near ready for production. Sales did not actually begin until a year later, and even then the car suffered from a number of teething troubles. However, it was the excellence of its basic design – with good handling, a gutsy engine and distinctive looks – which pulled it through. BMW followed the 1500 with a bored and stroked 1800 in 1964, distinguished externally by additional chrome trim, and with a twin-carburettor 1800TI which renewed the

public's taste for BMWs with high performance. A 1600 then replaced the 1500, and from 1966 there was a 2ltr 2000 as well, with a variant of the original 1500 engine which had initially been prepared for the 2000 and 2000CS coupés of 1965, which used the Neue Klasse's floorpan.

The Neue Klasse was also the car which ultimately fathered the 3 Series range. In 1966, it was cunningly developed into a short-wheelbase two-door model known initially as the '2 and later as the '02, and with this model's introduction BMW pushed the whole Neue Klasse four-door saloon range further up-market. The '02s took over the 1600 engine which then disappeared from the four-door range to leave the 1800 as the entry-level model. So it was that

With the big six-cylinder coupés of the late 1960s, known as the E9 models, BMW began to look like a serious challenger to the then-dominant Mercedes-Benz.

when the Neue Klasse finally retired in the early Seventies, it had given BMW a position in the medium saloon market with engines of 1800 and 2ltr capacity.

The Neue Klasse saloons all had derivatives of the same basic design of four-cylinder engine, but BMW knew it needed to move back into the big saloon sector and that to do this it would need a larger-capacity engine. So the next new range to appear – the 2500 and 2800 saloons of 1968 – was equipped with a big six-cylinder engine. BMW now had a much fuller range, beginning with the '02 models at the bottom, going on to the medium-sized four-door Neue Klasse cars, and culminating in the big-six

cars at the top. Coupé derivatives of these cars gave the company an exclusive, expensive, fourth range as well.

It was with this range – closely based on Mercedes-Benz practice – that BMW would enter the seventies. There was some shuffling of market positions, but the replacement ranges with their new model designations made the hierarchy even clearer. There would be 3 Series models as the smallest saloons, 5 Series cars as the medium range, 6 Series coupés and 7 Series big saloons – and that strategy has continued to the present day (although the 6 Series coupés were replaced by new flagship 8 Series cars in 1989).

The E12 medium-sized saloons of the first-generation 5 Series paved the way for the 3 Series cars to follow. This is a 1977 South African-built 518.

Based on the two-door '02 bodyshell, itself derived from the Neue Klasse four-door saloons, the 2002 turbo of 1973 was the world's first volume-production turbocharged car.

The Gallery of Contemporaries

Pictured here are some of the contemporaries of the 3 Series models.

The 6 Series coupés were introduced in 1976 to replace the big coupés with which BMW had gone racing in the early 1970s. These E24 models were suave and fast grand tourers.

The M535i featured Motorsport spoilers and suspension, but its engine was the same as in the standard E28 535i. The E28 medium-sized saloons lasted from 1981 to 1988.

The E31 8 Series coupés replaced the 6 Series models in 1989. This is an 840Ci Sport model, dating from the mid-1990s.

With the E32 7 Series, introduced in 1986, BMW went gunning for the top luxury car makers.

The third-generation 5 Series was the E34, introduced in 1988.

The E38 7 Series replaced the E32 models in 1994. Rivals Mercedes-Benz had failed to catch the mood of the time with their latest big and heavy-looking S-class, so the BMW was styled to look smaller and slimmer than it really was.

The E39 5 Series introduced in 1995 was widely acclaimed as the best family saloon in the world.

Meanwhile, BMW tackled the open roadster market in the mid-1990s with the Z3, built at the company's new US factory in Spartanburg.

THE '02 MODELS

As early as 1963, there had been discussions at BMW about a model which might fit in below the Neue Klasse saloons. In the beginning, this was conceived as a smaller car with an engine of around 1.4ltr, but the idea never seemed to be quite right.

So thoughts began to focus instead on a short-wheelbase two-door version of the Neue Klasse saloon. This plan had particular merit because the two-door car would help to re-establish the sporting image which BMW had enjoyed in the 1930s but had never recaptured since. The shorter wheelbase would also bring handling advantages while the lighter body would improve performance, and of course the two-door configuration would look more sporting than the four-door Neue Klasse type.

The two-door model did not take long to design. The Neue Klasse wheelbase was shortened from 100.4in to 98.4in, Wilhelm Hofmeister restyled the passenger cabin to suit, and the front of the car was given a minor facelift. Most of the running gear came directly from the existing four-door saloons, although there was a narrow-track rear axle which made front and rear tracks equal on the two-door model. BMW launched the car with the 1573cc '1600' engine in March 1966. For want of a more inspired name, they decided to call it a 1600-2 – the additional figure standing for its two doors and distinguishing it from the four-door saloon.

This was the car which opened up the market on which the 3 Series would later capitalize. Over an eleven-year production run, more than 860,000 two-door BMWs were built. There were convertible and hatchback 'Touring' versions as well as the basic two-door saloon. Engines ran from the original 1.6ltr type through a 1.8ltr and up to a 2ltr. The ultimate expression of the range was the 2002 turbo of 1973, justly famous as the world's first production turbocharged car – and the spiritual ancestor of the M3 models in the later 3 Series ranges.

2 First Generation – the E21 Models

When the first production E21-model BMW rolled off the production lines at the Milbertshofen factory in Germany on 2 May 1975, it marked the start of a new era. For although BMW had high hopes of its new two-door sports saloon, which replaced the highly-regarded '02 range – on sale since 1966 – the company's managers could not have anticipated just how successful the new models would be.

There were, of course, other factors affecting the company's production levels at the time, for the mid-1970s were a time of major expansion at BMW, but a look at output figures for the period shows the impact of the 3 Series quite clearly. In 1974, BMW built 184,330 cars. In 1975, boosted by 3 Series sales which had begun only in July that year, the total shot up to 221,298. For 1976, it went up again to 275,022; 1977 saw more than 290,000 and in 1978 it was up again, to over 320,000.

Production of most models of this first-generation 3 Series finished in November 1982, although the low-volume 315 model was still made up to the end of 1983. By then, more than 1.36 million E21s had been built. Of those, more than half had been

This head-on shot of a 316 model shows the clean lines developed for the cars.

This rear view of the same 316 demonstrates how the tail light units were neatly linked by a central black styling panel.

Core model of the first-generation 3 Series range was the 2ltr car. The original four-cylinder engine came with either carburettors or (as a 320i) with fuel injection, and was later replaced by a smooth six-cylinder type.

316 (1975–80)

Layout
Two-door saloon or Baur hardtop-cabriolet (1977–80)

Engine
Cylinders	Four
Bore × stroke	84mm × 71mm
Capacity	1563cc
Timing	Chain-driven ohc
Compression ratio	8.3:1
Carburettor	Solex 32/32 DIDTA
Max. power	90bhp at 6000rpm
Max. torque	90lb/ft at 4000rpm

Transmission
Gearbox	Four-speed manual	
Ratios	Normal	Optional three-speed automatic
First	3.764:1	2.478:1
Second	2.022:1	1.478:1
Third	1.320:1	1.000.1
Fourth	1.000:1	
Final drive	4.10:1	4.10:1

Suspension and Steering
Front	Independent suspension with MacPherson struts, coil springs and anti-roll bar
Rear	Semi-trailing arm suspension with coil springs and optional anti-roll bar
Steering	Rack and pinion with 19.0:1 ratio.
Wheels	5J × 13
Tyres	165 SR 13

Brakes
Type	Servo-assisted with dual hydraulic circuit
Size	Front 255mm discs
	Rear 250mm drums

Dimensions
Track	Front 1,364mm/53.7in
	Rear 1,377mm/54.2in
Wheelbase	2,563mm/100.9in
Overall length	4,355mm/171.5in
Overall width	1,610mm/63.4in
Overall height	1,380mm/54.3in
Unladen weight	1,040–1,060kg/2,293–2,337lb, depending on specification

The finely chiselled shape was very much of its time, but has worn well.

exported, doing immeasurable good for BMW's reputation in worldwide markets and paving the way for greater things in the future. It had been a most successful product, and one on which the company was able to build to great advantage with its successors.

It is rare for car companies to enter a market sector where they have not previously been represented, or to introduce a new model which creates its own market sector. With the E21 range, BMW was trying to do neither of these things. Instead, it was aiming to replace the '02 models which had taken the company into a new market during the 1960s. The '02s, derived from earlier compact family saloons, had tackled the small sports saloon market that had previously been the preserve of manu-

facturers like Alfa Romeo and Lancia. Their name was derived from the fact that they had just two doors instead of four, but their other chief characteristic was the driving pleasure they promised. With responsive, gutsy engines allied to slick gearboxes and sharp handling, these cars redefined the European understanding of a sports saloon. Reliability and durability boosted their desirability, and by the time they went out of production in the mid-1970s they had carved out for themselves a very special place in motoring history.

The '02s, then, were a hard act to follow. Yet they had a number of faults which BMW were determined to iron out in their successors. These included a lack of room in the rear (the cars were, after all, shortened versions of the earlier four-door Neue Klasse

---

318 (1975–80)

Layout
As for contemporary 316

Engine

Cylinders	Four
Bore × stroke	89mm × 71mm
Capacity	1754cc
Timing	Chain-driven ohc
Compression ratio	8.3:1
Carburettor	Solex 32/32 DIDTA
Max. power	98bhp at 5800rpm
Max. torque	105lb/ft at 4000rpm

Transmission
As for contemporary 316, except for 3.90:1 final drive.

Suspension and Steering
As for contemporary 316, except that rear anti-roll bar standard from March to August 1976 only

Brakes
As for comtemporary 316

Dimensions
As for contemporary 316

---

320 (1975–77)

Layout
As for contemporary 316; two-door saloon only

Engine

Cylinders	Four
Bore × stroke	89mm × 80mm
Capacity	1990cc
Timing	Chain-driven ohc
Compression ratio	8.1:1
Carburettor	Solex 32/32 DIDTA
Max. power	109bhp at 5800rpm
Max. torque	116lb/ft at 3700rpm

Transmission
As for contemporary 318

Suspension and Steering
As for contemporary 316, except that rear anti-roll bar standard from March 1976

Brakes
As for comtemporary 316

Dimensions
As for contemporary 316, except unladen weight 1,060–1,080kg/2,337–2,381lb, depending on specification

---

models) and a lamentable absence of ventilation in the passenger compartment when the windows were closed. Equally important when the design engineers in Munich settled down to work was that the '02s had been particularly popular in the USA, and that the new cars would have to pick up where they had left off. As the regulations governing passenger safety and exhaust emissions were growing tighter all the time in the USA, the new cars would also have to meet these.

One of the earliest decisions to be made by the engineers working under Bernhard Osswald was to make the new E21 models slightly larger than the '02s they would replace. While retaining the two-door configuration which would link them to the earlier cars and aid their sporting image, they would nevertheless have enough room inside to make them usable as family saloons. This would automatically broaden their appeal, as well as addressing the criticism levelled at the '02s that their interior space was inadequate. Thus, the E21s emerged as 3.5in longer and 0.8in wider than their predecessors, with a wheelbase that was 2.5in longer.

Inevitably, this made them slightly heavier as well. Yet the new bodyshell, which was of unitary constuction like that of the '02s, also managed to be around 18 per cent

Rear badging was discreet: there was just a BMW roundel in the centre of the boot lid, and a model designation on the right.

Four-cylinder E21s had single headlamps, but the six-cylinder cars were distinguished by paired lamps.

Instantly recognizable as a six-cylinder car because of its four headlamps, this is the top-of-the-range 323i.

stiffer. This in turn allowed improvements in suspension and handling, because a bodyshell which flexes too much works against the very best efforts of suspension engineers. Even more important for those customers whose priorities did not lie with the sporting elements of the BMW tradition, the new bodyshell made life in the back much more acceptable than before, by providing extra headroom, a longer cushion to give better thigh support and an extra 25mm (almost an inch) of extra knee room.

Invisibly, crash protection had been engineered into the shell, which had a rigid centre section and progressively deformable front and rear ends. The front-hinged bonnet was designed to bend in the middle rather than to penetrate the windscreen in an impact, and the centre of the car was protected by bracing between the B-pillars that effectively provided a roll-over bar. At

the rear, the fuel tank was relocated in the dead space underneath the rear seat, thus removing it from the vulnerable area at the tail of the car.

The styling of the new car was, of course, critically important, as it had to be clearly related to both the '02s and to other BMWs of the 1970s. The job of giving the new model contemporary lines fell to Paul Bracq, a French-born former Mercedes-Benz stylist who had joined the company at the beginning of the decade. He had already styled the crucially important E12 5 Series medium-sized saloons introduced in 1972, and his design for the E21 took on many of the elements of those cars. The reverse-slope front panel, the large glass area with thin pillars, and the angled trailing edge of the rear side window were existing BMW styling cues inherited from the designs done by Wilhelm Hofmeister in the 1960s.

To these, Bracq added strong horizontal lines, brightwork framing for the glass area and a stiff, angular D-pillar. Letterbox door handles and a side rubbing-strip which picked up the lines of the rubber-faced bumpers were further characteristics. In addition, Bracq came up with an particularly successful design of wheel that looked like a sporty alloy type and yet was actually pressed, far more cheaply, from steel. The overall result was distinctive and yet unostentatious – the sort of car which turned the heads of car enthusiasts but did not attract comment from anybody else.

Interior design was also carefully thought out. The E12 5 Series cars already had a neat and clear instrument panel with two main dials flanked a pair of smaller dials and underlined by a group of warning lights. The essence of this was carried over for the E21 models, but it was married to a new dashboard design which BMW called the cockpit style. This had a centre section angled towards the driver, bringing the minor controls closer to hand. On cheaper E21s (the 316, 318 and, later, 315) the second large dial on the main panel was a clock, but the more expensive models had a rev counter instead, and a smaller rectangular clock was fitted to the centre console. Red illumination of the white-on-black instruments gave a sporting feel, and was also quite distinctive among cars available at the time.

Characteristically German was the all-black plastic of the dashboard, which made the car look very spartan inside when black seats were fitted. However, an alternative beige interior relieved the mournful appearance and contrasted nicely with some of the bright exterior colours on offer. All seats came with PVC outer sections and cloth on the wearing surfaces, and the individual front seats always came with adjustable head restraints.

320i (1975–77) and US 320i (1976–80)

Layout
As for contemporary 316; two-door saloon only

Engine

Cylinders	Four
Bore × stroke	89mm × 80mm
Capacity	1990cc
Timing	Chain-driven ohc
Compression ratio	9.3:1
Fuel injection	Bosch K-Jetronic
Max. power	125bhp at 5700rpm
Max. torque	126lb/ft at 4350rpm

Transmission
As for contemporary 320, except for 3.64:1 final drive

Suspension and Steering

Suspension	As for contemporary 320, except standard rear anti-roll bar
Wheels	5.5J × 13 wheels
Tyres	185/70 HR 13

Brakes
As for contemporary 320

Dimensions

Track	Front 1,3486mm/54.6in
	Rear 1,399mm/55.1in
Wheelbase	2,563mm/100.9in
Overall length	4,355mm/171.5in (4,508mm/177.5in in USA)
Overall width	1,610mm/63.4in
Overall height	1,380mm/54.3in
Unladen weight	1,080kg/2,381lb

The suspension design was by no means new to BMW, but it was improved over that on earlier cars. Up front were MacPherson struts, now with a negative caster offset to improve stability. The A-arms used on the '02 models were replaced with simple lateral

The interior of an early E21 demonstrates the practical, functional layout. Even with the light-coloured seats seen here, however, the interior seems rather dark and uninspired.

In this department, however, the E21 excelled: the basic instrument layout is still used in the current 3 Series cars.

The E21 interior could look rather sombre, especially in the black which was commonly specified. Note the large four-spoke steering wheel in this four-cylinder car.

links, and the anti-roll bar acted as a bottom wishbone to locate the wheels fore-and-aft as in the original design patented by Earle MacPherson. At the rear, there was once again a coil-sprung semi-trailing arm system. The front springs were 25 per cent softer, with a stiffer anti-roll bar to compensate, while the rear springs were 40 per cent stiffer in order to reduce pitching. The roll centre of the rear suspension was slightly lower than before, but the semi-trailing arm suspension was still subject to sudden camber changes which could cause rear end breakaway. Perhaps BMW's view was that this characteristic added to the sporting nature of the car, or perhaps it would simply have been too expensive to redesign the suspension thoroughly at this stage. Either way, there were many less enthusiastic and less able 3 Series drivers who cursed the semi-trailing arms in later years when the rear end lost traction completely on a wet corner!

Steering was all new, too: a rack-and-pinion system made by ZF Gemmer. This was certainly cheaper than the worm-and-roller system used on the '02s, but it also

gave a degree of precision and feedback from the front wheels which added greatly to the sporting feel of the new car. Low gearing was specified to aid parking manoeuvres without the need for the cost and complication of power assistance, but this did make the response a little wooden at high speeds. On all models except for the entry-level 316, a hydraulic damper was fitted. As for the brakes, the vacuum servo gave 20 per cent more power than before, and this was allied to ventilated front discs with a 6 per cent increase in diameter and 60 per cent more friction area, and to rear drums which were around 9 per cent larger than before. In addition, a pressure-limiting valve was added to the rear hydraulic line for the first time.

On their introduction in 1975, the E21 models took on the new model-naming system which had been introduced with the 5 Series cars in 1972. These names consisted of three digits, the first representing the model range (3) and the second two representing the approximate size of the engine. Thus, the entry-level model with a 1.6ltr engine was called a 316, and above that came a 1.8ltr 318 and a 2ltr 320. In the beginning, the top of the range model was called the 320i – the terminal 'i' of course standing for the fuel injection which replaced the carburettor of the ordinary 320.

Right from the start, the 3 Series was a more prestigious car than the '02 which it replaced, and it sold at higher prices. Early press comment on the car makes clear that these prices seemed very high for the time, but the general feeling was that the high build quality and general excellence of the design more than made up for that. This was a sporting saloon which leapt immediately to the top of the class and, despite its wayward cornering behaviour in extremes, it was regarded as a car with admirable handling.

All those first cars had four-cylinder engines, with widely spread mountings and voids in the mounting blocks to give smoother running. However, it was consistent with BMW's pretensions for the 3 Series that a pair of six-cylinders should come to top out the range and to expand its appeal way beyond that of the '02 models. Further details of the new M60 six-cylinder engine are given on page 37; suffice it to say here that it arrived in September 1977 in the revised 320 model, which replaced both the original four-cylinder 320 and the injected 320i. A few months later, in February 1978, came an injected six of greater capacity for the new 323i. These engines, smooth and power-ful, were widely regarded as being among the best available anywhere in the world in the late 1970s.

Gearboxes were the next item to receive attention, when the original four-speed manual and three-speed automatic gearboxes were supplemented by optional close-ratio and overdrive five-speed types on the more expensive models from September 1979. After January 1982, the two six-cylinder models had five-speed gearboxes as stan-dard. Meanwhile, after injection had filtered down the range to turn the 318 into a 318i,

the 316 took on a 1.8ltr carburettor engine in place of its original 1.6ltr type. That change took place in August 1980, and was one of the early indications that the badging system would not always reflect engine capacity precisely, but might be dictated by marketing aims. The last new model to be introduced during the lifetime of the E21 range was the 315 in February 1981, and this used a detuned version of the 1.6ltr four-cylinder formerly in the 316. Trim levels were generally very spartan, and this model was also continued into the production era of the replacement E30 3 Series range in order to give a lower entry-level price to BMW ownership.

The 323i was distinguished by a neat black rubber boot lid spoiler as standard.

315 (1981–83)

Layout
Two-door saloon only

Engine

Cylinders	Four
Bore × stroke	84mm × 71mm
Capacity	1573cc
Timing	Chain-driven ohc
Compression ratio	9.5:1
Carburettor	Pierburg 1 B 2
Max. power	75bhp at 5800rpm
Max. torque	79lb/ft at 3200rpm

Transmission

Gearbox	Four-speed manual	
Ratios	Normal	Optional five-speed overdrive manual
First	3.764:1	3.681:1
Second	2.043:1	2.001:1
Third	1.320:1	1.329.1
Fourth	1.000:1	1.000:1
Fifth		0.805:1
Final drive	4.11:1	4.11:1

Suspension and Steering

Front	Independent suspension with MacPherson struts, coil springs and anti-roll bar
Rear	Semi-trailing arm suspension with coil springs
Steering	Rack and pinion with 21.1:1 ratio.
Wheels	5J × 13
Tyres	165 SR 13

Brakes

Type	Servo-assisted with dual hydraulic circuit
Size	Front 255mm discs
	Rear 250mm drums

Dimensions

Track	Front 1,366mm/53.8in
	Rear 1,373mm/54in
Wheelbase	2,563mm/100.9in
Overall length	4,355mm/171.5in
Overall width	1,610mm/63.4in
Overall height	1,380mm/54.3in
Unladen weight	1,050kg/2,315lb

All the E21 models built in BMW's Milbertshofen factory were two-door saloons, but from the end of 1977 until 1982 it was possible to buy a targa-top convertible model from BMW dealers. This was known to BMW as the Hardtop-Cabriolet derivative and, like its predecessor in the '02 range, it was actually converted by Karrosserie Baur in Stuttgart. The targa-topped '02 had been introduced in 1971 when many manufacturers believed that American safety legislation would eventually outlaw the full convertible, and its design was such a success that it was simply adapted for the 3 Series models.

The Hardtop-Cabriolet was a stylish design in which a rollover bar in the centre of the body was blended into the body sides just behind the doors. To improve its appearance, the sides of the bar were extended rearwards to incorporate quarter-light windows. The roof section above the front seats was made of plastic, and could be lifted out and stowed in the boot. Meanwhile, a folding cabriolet-type fabric hood over the rear seats could be lowered into a recess between the seats and the boot. Even though this design did not offer all the advantages of a true convertible, and even though the work put in by Baur raised the showroom cost quite alarmingly, the car managed to find around 3,000 buyers in five years of production.

THE ENGINES

The E21 models used variants of two basic engine families, the M10 four-cylinders and the M60 small-block six-cylinders. The M10 came in three different capacities, these being 1573cc in the 316 and later 315, 1766cc in the 318 and 318i, and 1990cc in the 320 and 320i. The M60, however, was available with only two different capacities: 1991cc in the 320 and 2315cc in the 323i. It is worth making the point that different capacities are sometimes quoted for these engines, but that those given here appear to be the definitive ones! Also worth noting is that the 320 was available first with a four-cylinder engine and then moved on to a six-cylinder and that, as a result, the two types are often known as 320/4 and 320/6 types.

The M10 four-cylinder engines were already well-known by the time they were introduced in the E21 3 Series cars. Their origins can be traced right back to 1958,

The early four-cylinder carburettor engine of a 316, 318 or 320. Note the transparent fusebox, a BMW feature.

316 (1980–82)

Layout
Two-door saloon or Baur hardtop-cabriolet

Engine

Cylinders	Four
Bore × stroke	89mm × 71mm
Capacity	1766cc
Timing	Chain-driven ohc
Compression ratio	9.5:1
Carburettor	Pierburg 2 B 4
Max. power	90bhp at 5500rpm
Max. torque	101lb/ft at 4000rpm

Transmission

Gearbox	Four-speed manual	
Ratios	Normal	Optional five-speed close-ratio manual
First	3.764:1	3.764:1
Second	2.043:1	2.325:1
Third	1.320:1	1.612.1
Fourth	1.000:1	1.229:1
Fifth		1.000:1
Final drive	3.91:1	3.91:1

For details of optional three-speed automatic *see* 316 (1975–80); for details of optional five-speed overdrive manual, *see* contemporary 315

Suspension and Steering

Front	Independent suspension with MacPherson struts, coil springs and anti-roll bar
Rear	Semi-trailing arm suspension with coil springs
Steering	Rack and pinion with 21.1:1 ratio.
Wheels	5J × 13, 5.5J × 13 optional
Tyres	165 SR 13

Brakes

Type	Servo-assisted with dual hydraulic circuit
Size	Front 255mm discs
	Rear 250mm drums

Dimensions

Track	Front 1,366mm/53.8in
	Rear 1,373mm/54in
Wheelbase	2,563mm/100.9in
Overall length	4,355mm/171.5in
Overall width	1,610mm/63.4in
Overall height	1,380mm/54.3in
Unladen weight	1,060–1,080kg/
	2,337–2,381lb, depending on specification

when Alex von Falkenhausen put forward a design for a 1ltr ohc four-cylinder engine, which he intended to be used in the forthcoming BMW 700 rear-engined car. That engine never went into production, but its design was resurrected when a 1.5ltr four-cylinder was needed for the Neue Klasse saloon. Thus, the first version of the M10 had a 1499cc capacity and appeared in the BMW 1500 saloon that was announced in 1961.

At that stage, BMW were entering a new era and could not predict with any degree of accuracy what engine capacities they might need in the future. Therefore, the M10 block was designed to be stretchable up to two litres, by enlarging both the bore and the stroke. It progressed through 1.6ltr and 1.8ltr sizes up to its 2ltr design limit in the Neue Klasse saloons and their two-door '02 derivatives during the 1960s and – just before the E21 3 Series cars went into production – it was also turbocharged for the legendary 2002 turbo. So the engine was thoroughly tried and tested by the time it went into the E21 models.

All variants of the engine had oversquare dimensions within a cast-iron block, while the cylinder head was made of aluminium alloy. There was a single overhead camshaft driven by duplex roller chain, and every M10 engine was canted over to the right by 30 degrees, thus allowing a lower bonnet-line than would have been possible if the engine had been installed upright. Fuel injection was first tried during the 1960s, but carburettors predominated in the E21 models.

There was a very clear hierarchy of power outputs and performance among the four-cylinder E21 engines. The 316 offered 90bhp and 100mph (161km/h), the 318 98bhp and 104mph (167km/h), and the 320 a very healthy 109bhp and 107mph (172km/h), all of them using the same Solex 32/32 DIDTA carburettor with automatic choke. The 320i, top of the range from 1975 until the six-cylinder models became available two years later, had Bosch K-Jetronic fuel injection and promised 125bhp, 113mph (182km/h) and much more useful acceleration in the gears.

The four-cylinder engines are represented here by the injected version in a 320i.

BMW took care over the presentation of the underbonnet scene. Note the cast intake manifold of this 323i engine, with its elegantly curving pipes.

318i (1980–82)

Layout
As for contemporary 316

Engine

Cylinders	Four
Bore × stroke	89mm × 71mm
Capacity	1754cc
Timing	Chain-driven ohc
Compression ratio	10.0:1
Fuel injection	Bosch Jetronic
Max. power	105bhp at 5800rpm
Max. torque	105lb/ft at 4500rpm

Transmission
Four-speed manual, three-speed automatic, five-speed overdrive manual or five-speed close-ratio manual, all with internal ratios and final drive ratios as for contemporary 316

Suspension and Steering
As for contemporary 316, except that rear anti-roll bar standard

Brakes
As for contemporary 316

Dimensions
As for contemporary 316, except unladen weight 1,070–1,090kg/2,359–2,403lb, depending on specification

K-Jetronic injection filtered down to the 1.8ltr models in 1980, when the 105bhp 318i took over from the carburetted 318. With a maximum speed of 108mph (174km/h) and much-improved acceleration, it was a much better car than its predecessor. As for the 315, which was introduced as an entry-level model only in 1981, it was deliberately de-tuned to give just 75bhp, although it could still haul itself up to 99mph (159km/h). By that stage, too, BMW were favouring the South African-built derivatives of Solex carburettors manufactured by Pierburg, and so the 315 had a Pierburg 1B2 carburettor.

Fuel injection was BMW's response to customer demand for improved performance in the 3 Series cars, and its efficient use of petrol also offered the most effective way of tuning engines to meet the increasingly tight exhaust emission regulations in the USA. However, even a highly efficient, highly tuned four-cylinder engine could not meet the other customer demand, which was for more refinement in the 3 Series. To tackle that, BMW turned to a new six-cylinder engine.

The existing M30 six-cylinder had been earning a solid reputation since its intro-

320 (1977–82)

Layout
Two-door saloon and (to 1981) Baur hardtop-cabriolet

Engine
Cylinders	Six
Bore × stroke	80mm × 66mm
Capacity	1990cc
Timing	Belt-driven ohc
Compression ratio	9.2:1
Carburettor	Solex 4A1
Max. power	122bhp at 6000rpm
Max. torque	118lb/ft at 4000rpm

Transmission
Four-speed manual or three speed automatic, both with internal ratios as for 316 and 3.64:1 final drive (1977–81); five-speed overdrive manual (ratios as for 315) with 3.64:1 final drive (from September 1979); five-speed close-ratio manual (ratios as for 316) with 3.45:1 final drive (from September 1979)

Suspension and Steering
Suspension	As for four-cylinder 320
Steering	Rack and pinion with 21.1:1 ratio; power assistance optional
Wheels	5J × 13
Tyres	155 HR 13

Brakes
As for contemporary 316

Dimensions
Track	Front 1,386mm/54.6in
	Rear 1,399mm/55.1in
Wheelbase	2,563mm/100.9in
Overall length	4,355mm/171.5in
Overall width	1,610mm/63.4in
Overall height	1,380mm/54.3in
Unladen weight	1,150–1,170kg/
	2,535–2,579lb, depending on specification

duction in 1968, but two factors made it unsuitable for the E21 models. Firstly, it had been designed for capacities of between 2.5 litres and 3.5 litres, which were incompatible with the market BMW were tackling with the 3 Series. Secondly, and decisively, it was physically too large to go into the engine bay of the E21.

Nevertheless, work had started on a small-block six-cylinder as early as 1971. This engine was designed for capacities of between 2 litres and 2.5 litres, and it was small enough to fit into the E21's engine bay. It had the same iron-block, alloy-head construction as the M10 four-cylinder engines, and it shared their 30-degree sideways

323i (1978–82)

Layout
Two-door saloon and Baur hardtop-cabriolet

Engine

Cylinders	Six
Bore × stroke	80mm × 76.8mm
Capacity	2315cc
Timing	Belt-driven ohc
Compression ratio	9.5:1
Fuel injection	Bosch K-Jetronic
Max. power	143bhp at 6000rpm
Max. torque	140lb/ft at 4500rpm

Transmission
As for six-cylinder 320, except for 3.45:1 final drive with all gearbox options

Suspension and Steering
As for six-cylinder 320

Brakes
As for six-cylinder 320, except for 258mm rear disk brakes

Dimensions
As for six-cylinder 320, except unladen weight 1,180–1,200kg/2,601–2,645lb, depending on specification

installation tilt. In place of a duplex chain drive for its single overhead camshaft, however, the M60 engine broke new ground by using a toothed rubber belt.

The M60 small-block six was introduced in 1977 in the 320 (where it replaced the 2ltr four-cylinder) and in the new top-of-the-range 323i. These designations indicated, of course, not only the capacities of nearly 2 litres and just over 2.3 litres, but also that the smaller engine had a carburettor while the larger, long-stroke type was fuel-injected. The 320 had a Solex 4A1 four-choke carburettor (which went on to earn a reputation as difficult to tune), while the

323i stuck to Bosch K-Jetronic injection. As refinement was the name of the game with the 320, the engine was tuned to give no more than 122bhp and 113mph (182km/h) – a vast improvement on the four-cylinder 320 and 320i models which it replaced, even so. The 2.3ltr engine, however, was tuned to make the 323i a proper road-rocket, with 143bhp giving a maximum speed of 119mph (191km/h) – quite shattering performance for a compact sports saloon in the late 1970s.

The M60 was silky smooth, too, if a little vocal in its more highly-tuned 323i guise. Until its introduction, the E21 3 Series had been lauded as more than usually competent; now, the range took on a completely new dimension. Without a doubt, this was the engine which established BMW's modern reputation for building top-notch six-cylinders. Overnight, it also realigned the 3 Series range by dividing it in two. From now on, there would be stolid and reliable four-cylinders for those who wanted the sporting cachet of the BMW marque but were not too demanding of performance. The sixes, however, would be the choice of driving enthusiasts.

GEARBOXES

Four different gearboxes were used in the E21 models, plus a fifth which was a variant of one of those four. A four-speed manual made for BMW by Getrag was standard on all the four-cylinder cars, and this was the one with two different variants. The original version was inherited from the '02 range, albeit with different second-speed gearing, and it was used in the 316 and 318 up to 1980, the four-cylinder 320, and the 320i. In addition, this gearbox was standard on the six-cylinder 320 from 1977 to 1981. With the second speed gearing changed yet again

Right at the end of E21 production, a special limited edition of around 200 323i models was built for UK dealers. This two-tone car is a surviving example of what is known to BMW enthusiasts as the 323i SE model, although it was never badged as such. The alloy wheels and tinted windows were standard 323i equipment.

(to 2.043:1 from 2.022:1), it was used in the 316 and 318i from 1980 to 1982, and in the 315 from 1981 to 1983. The second fuel crisis of 1979 had placed greater emphasis on fuel economy, and so this later version of the gearbox was developed to suit the higher axle ratios used in the later cars.

When the 323i was introduced in 1978, it brought with it two new gearboxes. Both were five-speed types, one being a close-ratio 'Sport' box with a direct top gear, and the other an overdrive type. Both were made available as options on the six-cylinder 320 from 1979, but the improved fuel economy available with the overdrive

five-speed made it the obvious choice when BMW needed to improve fuel consumption quickly to meet market demand after the 1979 oil crisis. So, from 1980, it appeared with the four-cylinder engines as well in the 316 and 318i; a year later it featured on the new 315 economy model as well.

The close-ratio Sport box, on the other hand, was designed to appeal to driving enthusiasts rather than economy-minded motorists. Once again made for BMW by Getrag, it always came with the same axle ratio as the overdrive gearbox, and thus offered quicker acceleration in the gears with a slightly lower maximum speed and higher fuel consumption. It followed the overdrive gearbox into the six-cylinder 320 from 1979, and then in 1980 found its way into the four-cylinder 316 and 318i as well. However, this gearbox was only available to special order, and the climate of the times ensured that it would always be one of the rarer options in the E21 range.

The final choice was a three-speed automatic gearbox bought in from ZF in Friedrichshafen. This was optional on every version of the E21 range except for the 315, and the internal gearing was always the same. Axle ratios, of course, varied to suit the torque of the engine, as the accompanying specification tables show. The 3 HP 22 gearbox, to use its full name, was brand-new in 1975 and had been developed specially by ZF to meet BMW's requirements. These included smoother shifts, which were achieved by dispensing with the old-fashioned brake bands of earlier BMW automatics and instead making the shifts through clutches. This operating system was already standard on US-built automatic gearboxes, but was new in Europe.

E21s for the US market were disfigured by extended bumpers. This is a 1980 320i which, despite its designation, actually had the 101bhp 1.8ltr four-cylinder engine.

OPTIONAL EQUIPMENT

In the days when the E21s were on sale, BMWs were advertised and priced with a basic specification, and it became something of a joke in the motor trade that almost everything was an extra-cost option. A radio was certainly not supplied as standard equipment, although few people actually bought their cars – particularly the more expensive variants – without one.

Inevitably, some of the more interesting options were standard in some markets on the top-model E21s. They included a slide-and-tilt metal sunroof, Mahle multi-spoke alloy wheels, a limited-slip differential, sports suspension (including Bilstein dampers) and Recaro sports seats for driver and passenger. In some markets such as the USA and Australia, an add-on air conditioning system was available. Although installed at the factory, this was not integrated into the dashboard, but had its outlet vents hung underneath, just ahead of the gear lever.

THE 320i FOR NORTH AMERICA

From the beginning of the E21's development, BMW had seen the USA and Canada as a very important market for the car. However, there was never any question of offering the full model-range to American buyers. The specifications demanded by US emissions and safety regulations were at this stage very different indeed from those suitable for the European countries which were BMW's largest markets, and to prepare a North American version of every 3 Series variant would have been ruinously expensive. So BMW decided to offer just one 3 Series model in the USA, where it would replace the much-loved 2002. That car was

introduced in 1976, and was badged as a 320i.

The North American 320i was of course broadly similar to the European car of the same name. However, its engine had been retuned to suit the unleaded fuel which was then becoming obligatory in the USA, and air injection, exhaust gas recirculation and a thermal reactor kept noxious exhaust emissions below the barriers imposed by law. The result was to stifle the engine somewhat and to affect performance, and the North American engine ran out of breath at around 6000rpm as compared to the 6500rpm of its European counterpart.

US 320i (1980–82)

Layout
Two-door saloon

Engine
Cylinders	Four
Bore × stroke	89mm × 71mm
Capacity	1754cc
Timing	Chain-driven ohc
Compression ratio	8.8:1
Fuel injection	Bosch Jetronic
Exhaust	Fitted with Lambda probe and three-way catalytic converter
Max. power	101bhp at 5800rpm
Max. torque	100 lb/ft at 4500rpm

Transmission
Five-speed overdrive manual as for contemporary 316, with 3.64:1 final drive

Suspension and Steering
As for contemporary 318i, but without rear anti-roll bar

Brakes
As for contemporary 318i

Dimensions
As for earlier US 320i

Production Totals

Four-cylinder E21

	316	318	318i	320	320i	315
1975	10,629	10,446		20,423	1,851	
1976	42,166	14,618		53,560	20,477	
1977	52,834	20,369		42,459	32,322	
1978	53,513	20,897		1,159	26,775	
1979	45,914	16,388	9,901	804	17,474	
1980	54,794	10,491	43,264			2
1981	44,019		71,739			33,115
1982	28,727		66,358			47,112
1983	4,438		1,302			27,069

Six-cylinder E21

	320	323i
1977	18,203	337
1978	61,402	18,467
1979	65,369	31,123
1980	59,383	36,424
1981	44,882	33,205
1982	21,206	17,851

Individual Model Totals

315	107,838
316	337,034
318	93,209
318i	192,564
320/4	118,399
320i	98,899
320/6	270,445
323i	137,107

Annual Production Figures

1975	43,349
1976	130,821
1977	166,758
1978	183,377
1979	188,809
1980	206,326
1981	228,832
1982	182,010
1983	33,757
TOTAL	1,364,039

CKD Production

Most E21 models were assembled in Germany, but in 1977 BMW began exporting CKD (Completely Knocked Down) kits for local assembly in Indonesia, Malaysia, South Africa, Thailand and Uruguay. The CKD figures given below are incorporated in the overall production totals given above.

1977	540
1978	1,164
1979	1,836
1980	1,968
1981	1,872
1982	756
1983	408
TOTAL	8,544

Nevertheless, with 110bhp (instead of the European 125bhp) it gave the car very good performance with some loss of the flexibility Americans had loved so much in the 2002.

The North American 320i was rather heavier than the European version, too. Most obviously, it was weighed down with the 5mph impact bumpers demanded by federal law, which protruded from each end of the car like a pair of ungainly shelves. Lighting regulations required that the front indicator lenses had to double as running lamps, and side markers were incorporated in the bumper wraparounds, but there was no need for the ugly additional light units which disfigured so many other European cars sold in the USA at this time. Inside, regulations demanded additional warning lights, one reminding driver or passenger to fasten the seat belt, and the other indicating that the EGR system was due for a service.

The cost of making the new small six-cylinder engine meet US emissions regulations meant that the 320i retained its four-cylinder engine after the European 320 had switched to the six. Then from 1980, the 2ltr four was replaced by a version of the injected 1.8ltr introduced that year in Europe. Yet the car retained its 320i badges, partly to deflect objections from the more enthusiastic segment of the BMW clientele: when the 530i had been replaced by a 528i in 1979, the press had complained bitterly that smaller engines were not what BMW enthusiasts expected. The change

was made mainly because the Corporate Average Fuel Economy standards introduced by the US Government in the wake of the 1979 oil crisis demanded much better fuel consumption, and the 1.8ltr engine delivered around 26 miles from every US gallon as against 21.5 miles from the 2ltr. Fitted with a three-way catalytic converter in the exhaust, it also met the latest emissions standards without the need for the air injection, exhaust gas recirculation, or thermal reactor which had adversely affected the driveability of the earlier car. So, despite a reduction in output to 101bhp, the 1.8ltr 320i pulled more cleanly and warmed up more quickly than its 2ltr predecessor. Equipped with the five-speed overdrive gearbox, the car promised 109mph (175km/h) – which was quite fast enough for North America at the time.

All the 320i models sold in the USA were two-door saloons; the Baur hardtop-cabriolet was not imported through official channels. However, a few examples of the latter did reach North America as personal imports. Similarly, the USA never officially had the E21 with a six-cylinder engine, although a few 320 and 323i models were imported by the US Alpina distributor and were made to meet emissions regulations before being sold on to customers. There were also several turbocharger conversions available from aftermarket specialists in the USA for those who insisted on getting more performance out of their 320i models.

3 Second Generation – the E30 Models

The BMW E30 3 Series was so closely associated with the booming world economies of the 1980s and the rise of the so-called 'Yuppie' class (Young, Upwardly-mobile Professionals) that it became something of an icon of its times. It was vastly more successful than the E21 3 Series which it replaced, more than two and a quarter million E30s being sold in thirteen years of production. Averaged out, E30 production gives a figure of nearly 180,000 cars a year, as compared to around 151,500 each year for the E21 models.

The E30s were introduced to the market in November 1982, production having begun a month earlier. Deliveries of the first cars commenced at the beginning of 1983, and the final saloon derivatives were built in

The four-door E30 was introduced in 1983, allowing BMW to compete on equal terms with the new Mercedes 190, which had been designed to steal sales from the 3 Series. Alloy wheels always improved the looks of the cars.

The E30s were instantly recognizable as BMWs from any angle, but they had more rounded styling than the E21s which had preceded them.

1991 after the third-generation E36 models had already been introduced. Yet other E30 derivatives – notably the cabriolet and Touring models – remained available into 1994. This allowed BMW more time to develop their E36 equivalents, and it was a marketing strategy which worked admirably well. The exclusive and specialist nature of these smaller-volume models ensured that they retained their appeal long after the basic saloons had become simply old models.

This expansion of the 3 Series range through additional models was an important factor in its success. The first cars came only as two-door saloons, like their E21 predecessors, but in spring 1983 BMW announced a four-door saloon which was designed to compete head-on with the new Mercedes 190 models. Over the years, sales of the two-door and four-door versions of the E30 would be roughly equal, the two-door appealing to the more sporting motorist and the four-door to

the family buyer. There were, of course, also some models made available with only one or the other bodyshell.

Baur hardtop-cabriolet versions of the six-cylinder 320i were available from 1982 to 1985, but at the 1985 Frankfurt Show BMW displayed their stunning new full cabriolet model. This entered series production in May 1986 and was always built at BMW's own factories. To the cabriolet and two-door and four-door saloons, the company next added an estate bodyshell in September 1987. This was badged as a 'Touring', the name recalling the hatchback 2002 Touring of a decade earlier, and in truth it was not very spacious as estate cars go. However, with the BMW cachet behind it, it found plenty of buyers who needed a little more space than was available in a standard saloon but did not want to trade down to a less prestigious marque to find it.

316 (1982–87)

Layout
Two-door saloon; four-door saloon from 1983

Engine

Cylinders	Four
Bore × stroke	89mm × 71mm
Capacity	1766cc
Timing	Chain-driven ohc
Compression ratio	9.5:1
Carburettor	Pierburg 2 B 4
Max. power	90bhp at 5500rpm
Max. torque	101lb/ft at 4000rpm

Transmission

Gearbox	Four-speed manual	Five-speed	Four-speed
Ratios	Normal	overdrive manual	automatic
First	3.76:1	3.72:1	2.48:1
Second	2.04:1	2.02:1	1.48:1
Third	1.32:1	1.32.1	1.00:1
Fourth	1.00:1	1.00:1	0.73:1
Fifth		0.80:1	
Final drive	3.91:1	3.64:1	3.91:1

Suspension and Steering

Front	Independent suspension with MacPherson struts, coil springs and anti-roll bar
Rear	Semi-trailing arm suspension with coil springs
Steering	Rack and pinion with 21.4:1 ratio; optional power steering with 20.5:1 ratio
Wheels	5J × 14; 5.5J × 14 from September 1985
Tyres	175/70 TR 14

Brakes

Type	Servo-assisted with dual hydraulic circuit; ABS optional from September 1986
Size	Front 255mm discs
	Rear 250mm drums

Dimensions

Track	Front 1,407mm/55.4in
	Rear 1,415mm/55.7in
Wheelbase	2,570mm/101.2in
Overall length	4,325mm/170.3in
Overall width	1,645mm/64.8in
Overall height	1,380mm/54.3in
Unladen weight	1,020–1,065kg/2,249–2,3347lb depending on specification

The Baur hardtop-cabriolet was based on a two-door model, and used a superstructure similar to that pioneered many years earlier on the 2002.

THE OPPOSITION

Yet the E30 3 Series did not have the market to itself. The E21 models had demonstrated that there was great sales potential for a compact saloon with sporting overtones, and Mercedes-Benz developed their new 190 models specifically to steal sales away from the successful 3 Series. Developments in the Mercedes line-up had a powerful influence on the way the E30s developed, and for a time in the 1980s it looked as if BMW was struggling to catch up. In the end, however, the two marques settled into their own familiar niches: the Mercedes 190 became the choice of the more staid and conventional buyer, while the

BMW 3 Series wielded a strong appeal to the sporting motorist.

The development of a four-door bodyshell to tackle the Mercedes threat has already been noted. Mercedes also fielded a diesel 190D, and so BMW responded in 1985 with versions of the E30 powered by the six-cylinder diesel engine they had developed mainly for the larger 5 Series models. These were only ever available in the four-door saloon shell, which indicated that they were thought of as 'sensible' cars! At the other extreme, Mercedes-Benz introduced a road-going version of their racing 190 in 1984, badged as a 190E 2.3-16. BMW responded with the astonishing Motorsport derivative of the E30 – the M3, which is discussed in

---

318i (1983–86)

Layout
Two-door and four-door saloons

Engine
Cylinders	Four
Bore × stroke	89mm × 71mm
Capacity	1766cc
Timing	Chain-driven ohc
Compression ratio	9.5:1
Fuel injection	Bosch L-Jetronic
Max. power	105bhp at 5800rpm
Max. torque	105lb/ft at 4500rpm

Transmission
Four-speed manual or five-speed overdrive manual, both with internal ratios as for 316 and 3.64:1 final drive; or four-speed overdrive automatic with internal ratios and final drive as for 316

Suspension and Steering
Suspension	As for contemporary 316
Wheels	5.5J × 14
Tyres	175/70 HR 14; 195/65 HR 14 from September 1985

Brakes
As for contemporary 316

Dimensions
As for contemporary 316, except unladen weight 1,020–1,090kg/2,249–2,403lb, depending on specification

---

320i (1983–86)

Layout
Two-door and four-door saloons; Baur hardtop-cabriolet

Engine
Cylinders	Six
Bore × stroke	80mm × 66mm
Capacity	1990cc
Timing	Belt-driven twin ohc
Compression ratio	9.8:1
Fuel injection	Bosch L-Jetronic
Max. power	125bhp at 5800rpm (129bhp at 6000rpm from September 1985)
Max. torque	123lb/ft at 4000rpm (126lb/ft at 4000rpm from September 1985)

Transmission
Five-speed overdrive manual (ratios as for contemporary 318i) with 3.45:1 final drive (3.91:1 final drive from September 1985); or four-speed overdrive automatic (ratios as for contemporary 316) with 3.46:1 final drive

Suspension and Steering
Suspension	As for contemporary 318i, except for rear anti-roll bar
Wheels	5.5J × 14
Tyres	195/60 or 195/65 HR 14

Brakes
As for contemporary 318i, except that ABS optional from 1983

Dimensions
As for contemporary 318i, except unladen weight 1,110–1,180g/2,447–2,601lb, depending on specification

---

more detail in the next chapter. This model was only available with two doors.

The E30 range was even influenced by developments at Audi, whose 1980 Quattro coupé had roused interest in four-wheel drive for road cars. Mercedes-Benz introduced its 4-Matic system for medium-sized saloons, but never offered it on the 190 range. BMW, keen to keep one step ahead, introduced four-wheel drive on the E30 with the top-model 2.5ltr engine in 1985, badging the result as a 325iX. Cost limited its

success, however, and BMW saved face by claiming that it was targeted mainly at buyers in Alpine regions, where four-wheel drive was a valuable safety feature. Like other low-volume models, the diesels and the M3, the 325iX was never made available with right-hand drive.

THE E30 TAKES SHAPE

BMW's engineers had started work on the E30 models as early as 1976, the same year in which Mercedes-Benz started work on their 190. These were the years when fuel economy had suddenly come to matter more than ever before, as a result of the 1973–74 Oil Crisis, and it was this which had led Mercedes to develop a compact saloon for the first time. For BMW, however, the issues were rather different. The company already had a successful model on its hands in the form of the E21 3 Series, and the main thrust of development was on updating and improving on that.

There was little doubt that the knowledge of future competition from Mercedes had a profound impact on the development of the E30 range, however. Build quality was a traditional Mercedes strength, and BMW was going to have to ensure that the new E30 was built to the very highest standards it could manage if the car were to be fully competitive. Equally, Mercedes was in many ways a conservative manufacturer, and the knowledge that the new 190 would not make any radically new advances in styling may have led BMW to decide against a major restyle of the 3 Series. One way or another, the E30 did not look very different from the E21 it replaced, although a neater nose treatment made it instantly recognizable.

Nor were there any major changes in dimensions. The wheelbase of the E30 was 7mm (2.75in) longer than that of the E21, while the overall length of the car came down by 30mm (12in). This inevitably pushed the wheels nearer the corners of the car, taking the layout nearer to the theoretical ideal of

---

323i (1983–85)

Layout
Two-door and four-door saloons; Baur hardtop-cabriolet

Engine

Cylinders	Six
Bore × stroke	80mm × 76.8mm
Capacity	2315cc
Timing	Belt-driven twin ohc
Compression ratio	9.8:1
Fuel injection	Bosch L-Jetronic
Max. power	139bhp at 5300rpm (150bhp at 6000rpm from September 1983)
Max. torque	148lb/ft at 4000rpm

Transmission

Gearbox	Five-speed overdrive manual	
Ratios	Normal five-speed	Close-ratio manual
First	3.83:1	3.764:1
Second	2.20:1	2.325:1
Third	1.40:1	1.612:1
Fourth	1.00:1	1.229:1
Fifth	0.81:1	1.000:1
Final drive	3.46:1	3.23:1

Four-speed overdrive automatic: ratios as for contemporary 320i with 3.23:1 final drive.

Suspension and Steering

Suspension	As for contemporary 320i.
Steering	As for contemporary 320i.
Wheels	5.5J × 14
Tyres	190/65 VR 14

Brakes
As for contemporary 320i, except for 258mm rear discs

Dimensions
As for contemporary 320i, except unladen weight 1140–1210kg/2513–2667lb, depending on specification

a wheel at each corner with no overhangs. Height was much the same as before, but an important change was made in the width, partly to acommodate wider tracks for better handling and partly to give more room inside. Weight was also reduced, mainly through the use of computer design to optimize the construction of the bodyshell, and the E30 models averaged some 88lb (40kg) less than the equivalent E21 models.

One of the main failings of the E21s had been their tendency to tail-happy handling. This was particularly apparent in the bigger-engined cars, and the BMW engineers set out to rid the E30s of this quirk. So, while they retained MacPherson strut front suspension (altering the position and diam-

The instrument layout in the E30 cars was both neat and functional.

eter of the anti-roll bar and making other small changes), they made some more fundamental changes at the rear. The trailing arms were mounted at 20 degrees (they had been at 15 degrees on the old car), and the coil spring and damper units were now mounted separately. The wider tracks made their own contribution, and the result was a car which was much less likely to break away in extreme conditions. The E30 would slide at the rear if pushed very hard, but the chances of this happening to an unwitting driver in everyday use were virtually eliminated. Steering now came with power assistance at extra cost, but both unassisted and power-assisted types were a little wooden in character.

Wheels on the E21s had been of 13in diameter, but BMW went up to 14in types as standard on the E30s. This was not just to suit lower-profile tyres; it also allowed larger-diameter brake discs for improved stopping power. Ventilated front discs were added for the six-cylinder cars (although the 323i would later revert to solid discs), but the rear brakes on all models except the 323i (and the more powerful models which followed later) were drums. ABS came only

Early cars had a four-spoke steering wheel, as seen here. Note how the seat belt is anchored to the bottom of the seat itself on this four-door model.

The interior of the E30s was still quite stark and functional, as this right-hand drive manual-transmission car shows. The three-spoke Motorsport wheel seen here was a popular option.

with the all-disc system, and was an extra-cost option, but on a car of this class it represented a leap ahead of most other manufacturers in the early 1980s.

The redesigned facia was a masterpiece, and added tremendously to the appeal of the car. Like the E21 type, it featured a central panel angled towards the driver. However, the air vents were now integrated into the top of this centre section to give better directional control and a neater appearance, and the main dials were cowled under a less angular binnacle. The standard four-spoke steering wheel was also less angular than the E21 type. Other interior items filtered down from the more expensive BMWs. These included an on-board computer (late in 1983), a fuel economy gauge and a service interval indicator. It all went to give the new models a more prestigious character, and the only real criticisms which could be levelled at these cars were the sombre nature of their interiors and the poor rear seat legroom. Later, lighter upholstery colours and a re-trimmed rear seat would go some way to alleviating these complaints.

BMW's own alloy wheels were a popular accessory on the E30 models.

This UK-market two-door E30 325i features both alloy wheels and a headlamp wash-wipe system.

Last but not least, BMW provided a whole range of extra-cost accessories which could push the otherwise quite reasonable show-room cost of an E30 into the stratosphere. Stylish alloy wheels were a great favourite. From the Motorsport division came the M-Technik aerodynamics kit of front and rear spoilers, the rear one matched by a marked curvature in the airdam on the boot lid. Side skirt extensions and a deeper rear apron could also be bought, and for real-world improvements there was an M-Technic sports suspension. This consisted of gas-filled dampers, stiffer springs and fatter anti-roll bars for front and rear. Cosmetically, it was matched by a leather-rimmed three-spoke steering wheel and a leather gear lever gaiter, plus BBS 6.5 × 14 alloy wheels. Buyers could also specify a limited-slip differential.

There were several modifications to the E30 range in autumn 1985; the mechanical changes are discussed later, but there were also many others, mainly designed to improve the car's aerodynamics. The 1986 and later E30s could be recognized by the smaller number of slots in their front spoilers, the smaller number of grille bars and – when steel wheels were specified – new, silver-grey plastic trims. A closer look would also reveal an engine undertray. Inside, there were changes, too. Most welcome was probably the improved lateral support of the standard front seats, while more visible was the switch from digital to analogue dashboard clock, and most practical the tougher anti-theft steering locks.

Further changes for the 1987 model-year saw the deletion of much of the bright metal

---

325i (1985–92)

Layout
Two-door and four-door saloons; cabriolet
(1986–92); Touring (1987–92)

Engine

Cylinders	Six
Bore × stroke	84mm × 75mm
Capacity	2494cc
Timing	Belt-driven twin ohc
Compression ratio	9.7:1
Fuel injection	Bosch ME-Motronic engine management system
Max. power	171bhp at 5800rpm
Max. torque	160lb/ft at 4300rpm

Transmission
Five-speed overdrive manual (ratios as for
323i) with 3.64:1 final drive (3.63:1 from
September 1987), or five-speed close-ratio
manual (ratios as for 323i) with 3.91:1 final
drive, or four-speed overdrive automatic
(ratios as for 323i) with 3.46:1 final drive

Suspension and Steering
As for 323i

Brakes
As for 323i

Dimensions
As for 323i, except unladen weight
1,190–1,350kg/2,693–2,976lb, depending
on specification

316i (1987–88)

Layout
Two-door and four-door saloons

Engine

Cylinders	Four
Bore × stroke	89mm × 71mm
Capacity	1766cc
Timing	Chain-driven ohc
Compression ratio	8.3:1
Fuel injection	Bosch L-Jetronic
Exhaust	Fitted with Lambda probe and three-way catalytic converter
Max. power	102bhp at 5800rpm
Max. torque	101lb/ft at 4000rpm

Transmission

Gearbox	Five-speed overdrive manual	
Ratios	Normal	Four-speed overdrive automatic
First	3.72:1	2.72:1
Second	2.02:1	1.56:1
Third	1.32.1	1.00:1
Fourth	1.00:1	0.73:1
Fifth	0.80:1	
Final drive	3.91:1	3.91:1

Suspension and Steering

Suspension	As for 316
Wheels	5.5J × 14
Tyres	195/65 HR 14

Brakes
As for 316

Dimensions
As for 316, except unladen weight
1,030–1,075kg/2,270–2,370lb, depending
on specification

---

on the body, especially around the side windows. At the same time, the bright steel bumper tops were replaced by plastic items painted in the body colour. These changes subtly updated the appearance of the E30s at minimum cost, and kept them looking fresh until the replacement E36 cars were introduced during 1990.

CABRIOLET AND TOURING

The E30 cabriolet actually entered production in January 1986, although a preproduction example had been displayed at

Sport and SE – UK-Market Specials

BMW's importers in several countries created their own variants of the basic E30s built in Germany by adding items from the options list. Typical of these were the Sport and SE (Special Equipment) models created by the UK importers. Neither type carried special badges, however.

The 325i Sport came with an M-Technic kit of spoilers and sports suspension, and with a limited-slip differential. Green-tinted glass was standard, together with sports seats like those on the big 635 coupé.

Typical of the SE models was the 320iSE. This came with power-assisted steering, alloy wheels, electric windows (front only on two-door variants), electric sunroof, on-board computer, headlamp wash-wipe, and a rear roller blind. Similar equipment was standard on the UK-market 325iSE model.

The British importers created their own special variants to improve sales. This is an E30 325i Sport.

the Frankfurt Show in autumn 1985. However, right-hand drive models did not make their appearance until the summer of 1986, production having begun in June.

The E30 cabriolet was remarkably free of the scuttle-shake and general body flexing which so often affects saloons that have been 'beheaded' which, in effect, this two-

The cabriolet was a handsome-looking car in side profile, and remains so today.

The cabriolet was a hugely desirable variant of the E30 range, and is much prized by enthusiasts nearly a decade and a half after it was introduced. Shown is a 320i.

door model had been. However, BMW had put a great deal of effort into reinforcing the body structure. Tougher side sills were fitted, and inside them were additional strengthening members. The floorpan was reinforced with thicker steel for the transmission tunnel and a double-skinned rear seat floorpan, while an extra steel plate was welded between rear side panels and rear inner wings.

There was even more reinforcement in the scuttle and under the dashboard. A bracing bar ran between steering column and transmission tunnel, extra panels were welded at the junction of side sills and A-pillars, and there were stiffening panels in

The flush-fitting hood well cover behind the rear seats was electrically operated on later E30 cabriolets. This UK-market model is a 320i or 325i.

the front wheelarches. Even the windscreen surround frame was of heavier gauge metal than on the E30s with a fixed roof.

Perhaps the most notable achievement of the E30 cabriolets, however, was the superb fit of their soft tops. BMW had been determined not to settle for anything less than the best, and had worked with established conversion specialists such as Karmann and Baur before settling on a design put forward by Shaer Waechter in Düsseldorf. No fewer

than six transverse hood bars and seven sticks per side made up the frame, and Teflon-seated bearings were used to ensure smooth action when the soft top was being raised or lowered. These bars tensioned the hood covering enough to eliminate the water leaks which are the bane of convertibles. As for the covering, it was of triple-layer sandwich construction, and did an excellent job of eliminating wind noise, except at higher speeds. The outer covering was of artificial

---

The 325i Motorsport Cabriolet

In 1990, BMW built a limited edition of 250 325i Motorsport cabriolets. To the basic 325i cabriolet, these cars added an M Technic body kit of front spoiler, rear skirts and side sills. Mirrors and bumpers were painted in the body colour of Sebring Grey or Macao Blue. The cars had uprated suspension with 7J × 15 cross-spoke alloy wheels with black-painted centres. The interior featured part-leather trim, with woven cloth for the wearing surfaces of the seats. The soft top was in black (with Sebring Grey paint) or blue, and the cars had the electro-hydraulic power-assisted soft top otherwise seen only on the M3 cabriolets.

316i (1987–94)

Layout
Two-door and four-door saloons (to 1991); Touring (1989–94)

Engine
Cylinders	Four
Bore × stroke	84mm × 72mm
Capacity	1596cc
Timing	Belt-driven ohc
Compression ratio	9.0:1
Fuel injection	Bosch Motronic
Exhaust	Fitted with Lambda probe and three-way catalytic converter
Max. power	100bhp at 5500rpm
Max. torque	102lb/ft at 4250rpm

Transmission
Gearbox	Five-speed overdrive manual	
Ratios	Normal	Four-speed overdrive automatic
First	3.72:1	2.73:1
Second	2.02:1	1.56:1
Third	1.32.1	1.00:1
Fourth	1.00:1	0.73:1
Fifth	0.81:1	
Final drive	4.10:1	4.45:1

Suspension and Steering
Suspension	As for 316, but with rear anti-roll bar
Wheels	5.5J × 14
Tyres	175/70 TR 14

Brakes
As for 316

Dimensions
As for 316, except unladen weight 1,100–1,200kg/2,425–2,667lb, depending on specification

---

fibres, the inner of cotton, and between them was a layer of sound-deadening (and waterproofing) rubber.

Not surprisingly, the weight of the extra body reinforcement coupled with that of the sturdy soft top and its framework made these cars heavier than their saloon equivalents. Performance was not greatly affected on the six-cylinder models that were the only cabriolets available in the beginning. However, the extra weight did make itself felt more on the four-cylinder 318i cabriolet introduced in 1990.

Just as happened with the cabriolet, the Touring was announced several months before it actually became available through the showrooms. A pre-production model was at the Frankfurt Show in September 1987, but production did not begin until March 1988.

Based on the more family-oriented four-door saloon, the Touring had reinforced body

The Touring estate may not have been very capacious, but it certainly had style. This alloy-wheeled example is a 325i.

A major fault with the Touring was the narrow entry to the load bay, caused by the large rear light clusters. This is a 318i model, with the stylish plastic wheel trims found on cheaper models.

<table>
<tr><td colspan="2">318i (1987–94)</td></tr>
<tr><td colspan="2">Layout</td></tr>
<tr><td colspan="2">Two-door and four-door saloons (1987–91);
cabriolet (1990–93); Touring (1989–94)</td></tr>
<tr><td colspan="2">Engine</td></tr>
<tr><td>Cylinders</td><td>Four</td></tr>
<tr><td>Bore × stroke</td><td>84mm × 81mm</td></tr>
<tr><td>Capacity</td><td>1796cc</td></tr>
<tr><td>Timing</td><td>Belt-driven ohc</td></tr>
<tr><td>Compression ratio</td><td>8.8:1</td></tr>
<tr><td>Fuel injection</td><td>Bosch Motronic</td></tr>
<tr><td>Exhaust</td><td>Fitted with Lambda probe and three-way catalytic converter</td></tr>
<tr><td>Max. power</td><td>113bhp at 5500rpm</td></tr>
<tr><td>Max. torque</td><td>117lb/ft at 4250rpm</td></tr>
<tr><td colspan="2">Transmission</td></tr>
<tr><td colspan="2">Five-speed overdrive manual (ratios as for contemporary 316) with 4.10:1 final drive, or four-speed overdrive automatic (ratios as for earlier 318i) with 4.45:1 final drive</td></tr>
<tr><td colspan="2">Suspension and Steering</td></tr>
<tr><td colspan="2">As for earlier 318i but with rear anti-roll bar</td></tr>
<tr><td colspan="2">Brakes</td></tr>
<tr><td colspan="2">As for earlier 318i</td></tr>
<tr><td colspan="2">Dimensions</td></tr>
<tr><td colspan="2">As for earlier 318i, except unladen weight 1,100–1,230kg/2,425–2,712lb, depending on specification</td></tr>
</table>

sides at the rear to carry the extra side glass and to compensate for the absence of a fixed transverse panel above floor level. Its tailgate was hinged at roof height, and had two low-pressure gas spring struts to assist opening and to support the panel in the open position. Despite the addition of an extra window on each side, the E30 Touring managed to avoid the frumpy look of many estate cars, and actually appeared quite stylish.

It had certain disadvantages, however. Weight was inevitably one of them, thanks to the body reinforcements needed at the rear. Load space was not enormous, partly because of the steeply-raked rear window used for styling reasons. Even though the rear seats could be folded forwards to extend the length of the load area, and even though the floor contained very practical lashing points, detractors pointed out that the narrow opening of the tailgate at floor height was far from ideal. Nevertheless, the Touring did make a practical occasional load-carrier, and BMW offered a self-levelling rear suspension option to maintain a constant ride height so that handling was not affected if the car was fully laden.

THE ENGINES

Over the thirteen years of their production, the E30 models used a far greater variety of engines than had the E21 models that preceded them. Although the entry-level 316 was introduced in 1982 with a carburettor engine, it lasted only until 1987 and every other petrol engine used in the E30 range had fuel injection. There were three basic families of four-cylinder engines (M10, M40 and M42), two basic families of six-cylinders (M60 and M20), and one six-cylinder diesel (M21). On top of that, there were the very special four-cylinder engines used in the M3 models, which are described in the next chapter.

Of the four-cylinders, only the 1766cc M10 was carried over from the E21 range. This chain-driven engine with its single overhead camshaft went into the 316 in carburettor form, and then into the 316i and 318i models equipped with fuel injection. The much smoother and more refined M40 was a completely new engine, developed for the E30 cars, and appeared with a 1596cc capacity in the 316i and in long-stroke 1796cc guise in the 318i. This had a belt-driven camshaft, but

The small-block six-cylinder M60 engine was in so many ways the real making of the E30 range. Early engines, like this one, came in 2ltr and 2.3ltr sizes. Later, there was a 2.5ltr edition as well.

Curved induction pipes distinguish the small-block M60 six-cylinder engine. This is the 2.5ltr version, in a 325i.

its M42 derivative, a four-valve derivative with twin overhead camshafts, reverted to chain-drive. The same 1796cc swept volume was used for this engine's only appearance, in the 318iS. With the exception of the Motorsport-developed engines in the M3 and Italian-market 320iS (*see* below), the M42 was the only four-valve type found in any E30 model, and it was not available in most countries.

318iS (1989–91)

Layout
Two-door and four-door saloons

Engine

Cylinders	Four
Bore × stroke	84mm × 81mm
Capacity	1796cc
Valves	Four per cylinder
Timing	Chain-driven twin ohc
Compression ratio	10.0:1
Fuel injection	Bosch Motronic M1/7 engine management system
Exhaust	Fitted with Lambda probe and three-way catalytic converter
Max. power	136bhp at 6000rpm
Max. torque	124lb/ft at 4600rpm

Transmission
Five-speed overdrive manual as for contemporary 318i

Suspension and Steering
As for contemporary 318i

Brakes
As for contemporary 318i, with 258mm rear discs

Dimensions
As for contemporary 318i, except unladen weight 1,135–1,106kg/2,502–2,557lb, depending on specification

320i (1986–92)

Layout
Two-door and four-door saloons (1986–91; Baur hardtop-cabriolet (1986 only); cabriolet (1986–92); Touring (1986–91)

Engine

Cylinders	Six
Bore × stroke	80mm × 66mm
Capacity	1990cc
Timing	Belt-driven twin ohc
Compression ratio	8.8:1
Fuel injection	Bosch Motronic
Exhaust	Lambda probe and three-way catalytic converter
Max. power	129bhp at 6000rpm
Max. torque	118lb/ft at 4300rpm

Transmission
Five-speed overdrive manual (ratios as for earlier 320i) with 4.10:1 final drive; or four-speed overdrive automatic (ratios as for earlier 320i) with 4.10:1 final drive

Suspension and Steering

Suspension	As for earlier 320i
Wheels	5.5J × 14
Tyres	195/65 HR 14

Brakes
As for earlier 320i

Dimensions
As for earlier 320i, except unladen weight 1,120–1,270kg/2,469–2,800lb, depending on specification

The M60 sixes with their belt-driven single overhead camshafts were carried over from the E21 models in 2ltr (1990cc) and 2.3ltr (2315cc) forms. Both shared the same 80mm bore dimension. The M20 sixes were newer types, again with belt-driven single overhead camshafts. They were introduced in 1985 in two forms, and once again had a common bore size, this time of 84mm. A 2494cc type was used in the 325i and 325iX models, while a special long-stroke version of 2693cc was used for the special 'eta' economy engine of the short-lived 325e. Lastly, the M21 diesels were belt-driven relatives of the M20 petrol sixes. They came with a 2443cc capacity, and were naturally aspirated in the 324d or turbocharged in the 324td.

The E30s were the first 3 Series models to be made available in Europe with catalytic

The 318iS was the only mainstream E30 to have a four-valve engine . . .

. . . which is seen here in a 1991 right-hand drive model.

converters to control exhaust emissions; these arrived on some models as early as 1984, but were standard on all models after 1986. Three fundamental changes in BMW engine technology also made themselves plain during the production life of the E30 models. First among them was the wholesale switch from chain-driven to belt-driven camshafts. Belt-driven camshafts had been previewed on the M60 small-block six in the

E21 cars, but every other engine then on offer had a chain drive. By contrast, every engine used in the E30 range used a belt drive, except for the 1766cc M10 types, which ceased production during 1987.

The second fundamental change was a similar wholesale switch to fuel injection. While fuel injection had been new and exciting on the E21 cars, by the time of the E30s it was very much expected. Only the 316 model retained a carburettor engine, and that – the elderly M10 four-cylinder – went out of production in 1987. The third change in engine technology was the arrival of four-valve cylinder heads. Introduced by the Motorsport division on the more expensive and exotic BMWs towards the end of the 1970s, they spread to the E30s through the M3 in the mid-1980s, and then to the 318iS in 1989. The 1796cc four-cylinder engine in the 318iS and the very special engine in the Italian-market 320iS were the only four-valve types in the range outside the M3, but they proved to be heralds of the engine designs which would appear in the next generation of 3 Series BMWs – the E36 models announced in 1990.

With the E30s, the power and performance hierarchy was rather less clear than it had been with the E21s. There were three reasons for this. The first was that the 2.4ltr diesel engines in the 324d and 324td did not offer more power than the 323i which was numerically below them in the range. The second was that the 122bhp of the economy-model 325e was lower than the 125bhp of the 320i, and the third was that the 318iS with its 136bhp four-cylinder offered more performance than the contemporary 129bhp six-cylinder 320i.

That said, there was a spread of power and performance from the 90bhp of the original four-cylinder 316 to the 171bhp of the six-cylinder 325i. The 316 always offered the same power, with a very respectable top

The diesel-engined 324td was distinguished from the 324d by its turbocharger, and by this badging.

speed of 109mph (175km/h). The later 316i, with its 100bhp fuel-injected M40 engine, promised 115mph (185km/h), but its acceleration through the gears was much the same.

The 318i models presented a bewildering variety. The original car without catalytic converter had 105bhp and 115mph (185km/h), but the M10-engined model with a catalyst had 102bhp and a top speed of just 112mph (180km/h). The same engine was then used in the 316i model for 1987–88, while the 318i switched to a 113bhp M40 engine which promised 118mph (190km/h). The four-valve 318iS was a completely different kettle of fish, with 136bhp, a top speed of 127mph (204km/h), and a 0–60mph (97km/h) sprint time of under 10 seconds.

The six-cylinders started with the 320i, which initially had 125bhp and then 129bhp from 1987; both versions had a top speed of 124mph (200km/h). The 323i started with 139bhp but was uprated to 150bhp in 1983; even so, BMW claimed the same 127mph (204km/h) top speed for both versions. The top-of-the-range 325i with 171bhp (or 170bhp with catalyst) was a 136mph (219km/h)

325e (1985–86)

Layout
Two-door and four-door saloons; Baur hardtop-cabriolet

Engine

Cylinders	Six
Bore × stroke	84mm × 81mm
Capacity	2693cc
Timing	Belt-driven twin ohc
Compression ratio	11:1
Fuel injection	Bosch Motronic engine management system
Exhaust	Fitted with Lambda probe and three-way catalytic convertor
Max. power	122bhp at 4250rpm
Max. torque	166lb/ft at 3250rpm

Transmission
Five-speed overdrive manual (ratios as for 324d) with 2.93:1 final drive

Suspension and Steering

Suspension	As for 320i
Steering	As for 320i
Wheels	5.5J × 14
Tyres	195/65 HR 14

Brakes
As for 320i

Dimensions
As for 320i, except unladen weight 1,170–1,240kg/2,579–2,734lb, depending on specification.

324d (1985–91)

Layout
Four-door saloon only

Engine

Cylinders	Six
Bore × stroke	80mm × 81mm
Capacity	2443cc
Timing	Belt-driven twin ohc
Compression ratio	22.1:1
Fuel injection	Mechanical; electronic from March 1989
Max. power	86bhp at 4600rpm
Max. torque	110lb/ft at 2500rpm

Transmission
Five-speed overdrive manual (ratios as for 1983–87 316) with 3.45:1 final drive, or four-speed overdrive automatic (ratios as for 316i) with 3.23:1 or 3.45:1 final drive.

Suspension and Steering

Suspension	As for 1983–87 316
Steering	As for 1983–87 316
Wheels	5.5J × 14
Tyres	175/70 TR 14

Brakes
As for 1983–87 316, but no ABS option

Dimensions
As for 1983–87 316, except unladen weight 1,220–1,240kg/2,690–2,734lb, depending on specification

---

motor car, although the maximum dropped as low as 127mph in the four-wheel drive 325iX with catalytic converter.

UNUSUAL DEVELOPMENTS

Out on a limb were the 325e and the diesels. With 122bhp, the 325e engine was tuned for fuel economy, and the car's gearing promoted this rather than rapid acceleration. Nevertheless, a 325e was no slouch, with a 118mph (190km/h) top speed. The naturally-aspirated 324d had just 86bhp and was aimed primarily at the taxi trade and the economy-minded, neither of whom objected to its lowly 105mph (169km/h) maximum. The turbocharged 324td with 115bhp was a much better bet, however, and gave a respectable maximum of 115mph (185km/h).

These new engines were interesting symbols of their age, when fuel economy had become a very significant factor in new car sales. Developed primarily as an economy engine for the bigger E28 5 Series saloons, the 2693cc M20 engine in the 325e was a long-stroke version of the six-cylinder which powered the high-performance 325i. It was known as the 'eta' type, 'eta' being the Greek letter E, which is used by engineers to represent efficiency.

The 'eta' engine did not rev as high as the other BMW sixes, and was tuned to develop high torque at much lower crankshaft speeds. This reduced the frictional losses which cost fuel, and economy was further aided by the precise fuel metering made possible by the latest Bosch L-Jetronic fuel injection system. An ultra-high compression ratio of 11:1 also aided economy.

It was a brilliant concept, and went down well in the USA, where the engine was first introduced in the E28 528e during 1982. In that territory, it remained available until as late as 1989 in the 325e model (which was later renamed as a plain 325). In Europe, however, the 325e was a comparative failure. Customers there had a wider choice of E30 models, and were unwilling to pay extra for the refinement of a large six-cylinder engine which was no more economical than a cheaper four-cylinder, and offered nothing more in the way of performance. Calling it a 325e rather than the more logical 327e did nothing to dispel the idea that this was a big-engined and therefore thirsty car, so the European 325e version of the E30 was withdrawn from sale in 1987, after only a year in the showrooms.

The M21 diesels were also reflections of BMW's preoccupation with fuel economy after the shock of the 1973–74 oil crisis. Developed from the M60 small-block six-cylinder petrol engines, these had indirect

---

324td (1987–91)

Layout
Four-door saloon; Touring

Engine

Cylinders	Six
Bore × stroke	80mm × 81mm
Capacity	2443cc
Timing	Belt-driven twin ohc
Compression ratio	22.1:1
Fuel injection	Electronic
Exhaust	Catalytic converter optional from spring 1980
Turbocharger	Garrett exhaust-druven
Max. power	115bhp at 4800rpm
Max. torque	160lb/ft at 2400rpm

Transmission

Gearbox	Five-speed overdrive manual
Ratios	
First	3.83:1
Second	2.20:1
Third	1.40:1
Fourth	1.00:1
Fifth	0.81:1
Final drive	3.25:1

(Four-speed overdrive automatic (ratios as for 324d) with 3.25:1 final drive)

Suspension and Steering

Suspension	As for 324d
Steering	As for 324d, but power-assisted steering standard
Wheels	5.5J × 14
Tyres	195/65 HR 14

Brakes
As for 324d, but with 258mm rear discs

Dimensions
As for 324d, except unladen weight 1,270–1,350kg/2,800–2,976lb, depending on specification

injection and Ricardo-type swirl chambers to aid economy. Although the first viable prototype engines were running as early as 1978, delays in getting them into production prevented their introduction before 1983. The engines were always intended to offer performance as well as the traditional diesel economy, and to that end they were designed for use with a turbocharger.

The engine first appeared as a turbocharged type in the E28 5 Series models, and the same engine was introduced to the E30 range four years later in the 324td. In the meantime, however, 1985 had seen the arrival of a non-turbocharged version in the 324d. This less powerful engine aided differentiation between the 3 Series and more expensive 5 Series ranges. However, its performance was disappointing by BMW standards. The turbocharged engine, by contrast, gained a strong following. The non-turbocharged engine was withdrawn from production when the E36 3 Series models replaced the E30 range in 1991, but

---

The 325iX and Four-Wheel Drive

The four-wheel drive system fitted to the 325iX was a sophisticated system based on Ferguson patents which had been bought by GKN in Britain. The system was manufactured by an Anglo-German co-operative, and was essentially the same as was sold to Ford for their four-wheel drive cars of the time. BMW arranged for the power to be split unequally between front and rear, 63 per cent going to the rear wheels, so that the 325iX retained the handling characteristics of the rear-wheel drive car on which it was based.

The transmission system added a viscous coupling behind the primary gearbox, together with a transfer gearbox and a central differential. From the transfer box, an exposed propellor shaft driven by a multiple-row Morse chain took drive forward to the front wheels, passing the engine on the left-hand side and necessitating a modified sump. A front differential turned the drive round through 90 degrees, and a single drive-shaft then took it to each front wheel.

The extra drivetrain components necessitated some alterations to the front suspension as well, which was mounted on a special sub-frame. The 325iX had special aluminium lower wishbones and repositioned struts giving negative-offset geometry. The anti-roll bar and certain steering components were repositioned, and the front cross-member was relocated further forwards. All this extra hardware caused the 325iX to ride a little higher than a standard 325i. It also made the car heavier, and power losses through the additional drivetrain components tended to make the 325iX rather slower than the equivalent two-wheel drive model.

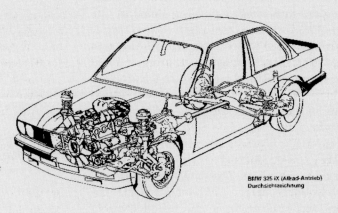

For the 325iX, BMW developed a special all-wheel drive system. This cutaway drawing shows the main elements of the powertrain.

BMW 325 iX (Allrad-Antrieb)
Durchsichtzeichnung

---

a further-developed turbocharged diesel was kept on the 3 Series options list.

GEARBOXES

Leaving aside the M3 models, the E30 range used four different gearboxes. The most common types were five-speed overdrive manuals and the four-speed overdrive automatics which were their optional alternatives. These overdrive ratios of course reflected BMW's preoccupation with fuel economy. A four-speed manual was standard on the carburettor 316 and on the early 318i, but ceased production in 1986. The final choice was a five-speed close-ratio Sport gearbox, available only on the 323i, 325i and 325iX models.

The Getrag-built four-speed manual was carried over from the E21 models, and used a familiar set of gear ratios. The overdrive five-speed manual had made its debut in 1978 on the six-cylinder E21s, but was now available across the range. It came with two different sets of internal ratios. One was used with all the four-cylinder engines, on the 320i, 324d and 325e. The other, which had lower first, second, third and fifth ratios, was specified for the 323i, 324td, 325i and 325iX. As for the close-ratio Sport gearbox, this too had first been seen in the high-performance models of the E21 range in 1978.

LIke the earlier three-speed automatic used in the E21 models, the new four-speed automatic was made by ZF at Friedrichshafen. Known as the 4HP22, this was a pioneering design which offered both smooth change quality and an overdrive top gear that promised much better fuel economy than had been available with earlier automatics. One of its outstanding features was that the torque converter locked up above 53mph/85km/h (although

---

325iX (1985–92)

All specification details as for 325i, except as follows:

Drivetrain
Permanent four-wheel drive, with centre differential giving a torque split of 37 per cent to the front wheels and 63 per cent to the rear wheels; viscous limited-slip centre and rear differentials

Final drive
3.91:1 with both types of five-speed manual gearbox, or 3.73:1 with four-speed automatic

Suspension and Steering
Steering   Power assistance standard
Wheels   6J × 14 wheels
Tyres   195/65 VR 14 tyres
Option   365 × 150 TD alloy wheels
             with 200/60 VR 365 tyres

Brakes
ABS system standard

Dimensions
Track   Front 1,420mm/55.9in
              Rear 1,416mm/55.7in
Overall height 1,400mm/55.1in
Unladen weight 1,270–1,430kg/
              2,800–3,152lb, depending
              on specification.

---

the speed was higher under hard acceleration), to prevent the fuel-wasting slip which had always been a feature of older automatic gearboxes. A good degree of manual override was also available, and this made the gearbox far more attractive than earlier types to enthusiastic drivers.

THE E30 IN THE USA

As they had done with the E21 range, BMW made a careful selection of E30 models for

In the USA, a 325i was used as a test-bed to prove the properties of the new Mobil 1 engine oil; it was run for 1,000,000 miles without problems. Note the deep spoiler associated with the big-engined car – which in this case is a two-door model – and the US-specification side marker lights in the bumper.

sale in the USA. The 318i was chosen to represent the four-cylinder models, and the 325e was the initial choice to represent the six-cylinder types. Both, however, were different from models of the same name sold in other countries.

The 318i had the 1766cc M10 engine from the earlier US-model E21 320i. Still developing the same 101bhp, and driving through a five-speed overdrive gearbox, it would take the new car to a top speed of 113mph (182km/h). In this, it was much the same as its catalyst-equipped European equivalent, but BMW buyers in the USA demanded an all-disc braking system. In Europe, this was not available on any four-cylinder model at the time, and rear discs were only specified on the high-performance 323i and larger-engined models. Not until 1989 did a European four-cylinder E30 get disc brakes on the rear wheels – and that was the 318iS which was a much faster car than the US-model 318i.

The six-cylinder model was the economy-tuned 325e with the 122bhp 2.7ltr 'eta' engine, and this could run to 116mph (187km/h). Two-door versions arrived in 1984 to establish a sporting image before the four-door companion model was introduced in 1985. A year later, BMW split the six-cylinder range into three. All used the same engine, but the base model was renamed a 325. The 325e designation was now reserved for a luxury-trim version of the four-door car, with leather upholstery and ABS as standard. The third variety was based on the two-door shell, and was equipped as a sporty model with spoilers and other items. This was known as the325es.

There were further changes for 1987. The base-model 325 stayed with the 'eta' engine, but the 325e and 325es were replaced by a 325i and 325is with the 2.5ltr six-cylinder engine and a lot more performance. The 325i was the luxury-trim model, and the 325is the sporty variant. They were also joined by a 325i convertible which was essentially, of course, the European 325i cabriolet. The final range revision came in 1988, when the four-wheel drive 325iX was added to the line-up of 318i, 325, 325i and 325is.

THE SOUTH AFRICAN 333i

Specialist tuner Alpina had already shown that it was possible to drop BMW's big six-cylinder engine into the E30 3 Series in its B6 conversion. Out in South Africa, the management of BMW's assembly plant decided to make a similar car as a low-volume, line-produced model for domestic consumption. The engineering work needed was overseen by Bernd Pischetrieder, who later became BMW's Chairman.

The 333i actually used a number of Alpina parts, specially imported from

Germany, and these included the Alpina instrument pack and multi-spoke 7x16 alloy wheels. The car was decked out with a Motorsport front air dam and with the boot spoiler from the 323i, and had special badging with the Motorsport tricolour as a background.

BMW South Africa believe about 220 examples of the car were built at its Rosslyn plant. They were sold only in South Africa, although a few reached Britain and Hong Kong as personal imports. All of them had the two-door bodyshell, and all of them had right-hand drive.

THE ITALIAN 320iS

In Italy, petrol engines with a larger capacity than two litres suffer heavy taxation. BMW reasoned that the high-performance derivatives of their 3 Series cars had to compete with the home-grown

---

South African 333i (1985-1987)

Engine
Cylinders	Six
Bore × stroke	89mm × 86mm
Capacity	3210cc
Max. power	197bhp at 5500rpm
Max. torque	210lb/ft at 4300rpm

Transmission
Five-speed close-ratio manual gearbox; no automatic option; limited-slip differential

Steering
Power-assisted steering standard

Brakes
Ventilated rear disc brakes and ABS standard; 296mm Alpina ventilated and slotted front discs optional

Wheels and Tyres
7J × 16 Alpina alloy wheels with 195/50 VR 16 tyres

320iS

Engine
Cylinders	Four, with four valves per cylinder
Bore × stroke	93.4mm × 72.6mm
Capacity	1990cc
Max. power	192bhp at 6900rpm

Transmission
Five-speed manual gearbox; no automatic option

Brakes
Disc brakes on the rear wheels instead of standard model's drums

Performance
Max. speed   141mph/227km/h (two-door); 0–62mph (0–100km/h) in 7.9sec

2ltr from the likes of Alfa Romeo, and the standard 129bhp engine in the 320i was simply not up to the task. Therefore, a special engine was developed and made available only in Italy.

BMW turned to their Motorsport division for a solution, and the result was a short-stroke, 2ltr edition of the four-valve M3 engine. It was, of course, only a four-cylinder rather than a silky six like the engine in the regular 320i, but it went so well that nobody seemed to lament the absent refinement and absent cylinders. To distinguish the re-engined car from the existing 320i, it was badged as a 320iS, and it carried the full complement of Motorsport spoilers and other addenda.

Having the four-valve 2ltr engine in production also allowed BMW to use it in Class 2 racing events. There were just 2,540 two-door 320iS models, and 1,205 four-door types, all of them sold in Italy.

Production totals

Four-cylinder E30

	316	316i	318i	318iS
1982	1,199		2,339	
1983	37,536		76,387	
1984	65,185		75,535	
1985	59,053		78,295	
1986	63,699		50,146	
1987	46,888		26,302	
1988		54,122		
1989		75,181		
1990		63,361		9,442
1991		1,337		29,171
1992				2,621

Six-cylinder E30

	320i	323i	325i	325iX	325e
1982	7,134	4,909			
1983	64,766	32,611			872
1984	65,444	33,411			25,471
1985	46,010	18,538	13,686		59,832
1986	36,227	1,307	32,195		77,317
1987	61,606		52,958		22,393
1988	38,306		43,280	4,203	3,402
1989	33,949		30,035	4,047	
1990	26,427		23,179	2,256	
1991	901		1,603	36	

Six-cylinder Diesel E30

	324d	324td
1985	10,583	
1986	35,562	
1987	17,800	7,261
1988	5,259	7,029
1989	3,729	4,251
1990	2,763	2,973

Motorsport E30s: 320iS and M3

	320iS	M3
1985		1
1986		2,396
1987	11	6,396
1988	2,419	3,426
1989	624	2,541
1990	691	2,424

Individual Model Totals

316	273,560
316i	194,001
318i	309,004
318iS	41,234
320i	380,770
320iS	3,745
323i	90,776
324d	75,696
324td	21,514
325i	196,936
325iX	10,542
325e	189,287
M3	17,184

Annual Production Figures

	1982	1983	1984	1985	1986	1987	1988
Saloon	15,580	212,172	265,046	286,895	305,651	274,529	212,936
Cabrio				11	10,791	26,674	21,145
Touring						16	17,412
Total	15,580	212,172	265,046	286,906	316,442	301,219	251,493

	1989	1990	1991	1992	1993	1994	Total
Saloon	200,654	184,999	8,899				1,967,361
Cabrio	20,747	21,964	23,679	16,233	2,181		143,425
Touring	20,714	23,427	13,199	10,680	16,259	1,997	103,704
Total	242,115	230,390	45,777	26,913	18,440	1,997	**2,214,490**

CKD Production

CKD production for overseas markets expanded enormously during the lifetime of the E30 models, as a comparison with the figures for E21 models (see page 46) shows. E30s were assembled in the same five overseas plants which had assembled the E21s. The CKD figures given below are additional to the production totals given above.

1983	6,029
1984	20,088
1986	13,020
1987	14,856
1988	17,582
1989	15,192
1990	16,428
1991	10,596
1995	10,980
TOTAL	124,771

Grand total of E30 production: 2,339,261

4 The Mighty M3

Few cars announced during the 1980s had anything like the impact on the popular imagination of the original BMW M3.

The M3 badge was discreet, but it quickly became a symbol of BMW's success.

Announced in 1985 but not available until a year after that, this version of the E30 3 Series brought the glamour and performance of the special cars from BMW's Motorsport division down to a more affordable level. The M3 was never a cheap car, of course – far from it – but it did become massively successful and at the same time it became a benchmark for every high-performance compact saloon for years to come.

The original M3, then, was a landmark car – and there are many who would argue that it will always be the greatest of the BMWs to bear that name. Subsequent M3s, in the E36 and E46 ranges, have introduced a greater degree of refinement which makes them markedly different from the raw, fire-breathing E30 version.

Flared wings over alloy wheels and spoilers front and rear made it easy to distingush the M3 from lesser E30s, although the car was in other respects very similar to them.

ORIGINS

Although it is quite true that the M3 was developed largely to further BMW's competition aims in the mid-1980s, there is rather more to its story than that. The origins of the car which was to become the M3 lie much further back, at the turn of the decade, before the mainstream E30 models had even entered production. The need to revive the BMW name in touring car events nevertheless added a certain impetus to the project during its later stages, and the decision to take the car racing was the main reason for some elements of the production design. Once the BMW reputation had been re-established in touring car racing (*see* Chapter 9), the car's competition career also gave rise to some particularly interesting limited-edition variants.

First of all, it is important to understand the role of the BMW Motorsport division within BMW as a whole. Established in 1972 to look after the company's competitions programme, it was initially run by Jochen Neerpasch. From 1973, it had its own distinctive corporate livery of blue, violet and red stripes, and later on these would be used alongside a chromed capital M as the division's logo. From the beginning, the Motorsport division prepared competition BMWs for private entrants, as well as for

This was the car the M3 had to beat. Mercedes' 190E 2.3-16 had a Cosworth-developed four-valve engine and was designed to win racetrack honours for its makers. At the Nurburgring in May 1984, a young Ayrton Senna is seen here leading the field of Formula 1 drivers in a one-marque race.

the BMW works team, and before long it turned its hand also to the construction of one-off specials for senior BMW officials and other favoured customers.

Therefore, when BMW wanted to create a mid-engined supercar which would beat Porsche in track events, it naturally turned to its own Motorsport division to design and develop the car. Any car which was to represent its manufacturer in the popular FISA events of the time had to be 'homologated' – approved by a FISA committee – and one of the requirements of homologation was that a minimum number of examples should be built. So the Motorsport division's mid-engined supercar became the BMW M1 and was offered for sale to the public in order to justify (and finance) the required number of examples. For a variety of reasons which are of no interest here, the M1 never did fulfil BMW's expectations on the track. However, it did establish the M-badged Motorsport cars as a brand, which swiftly expanded through the relatively tame E12 M535i of 1979 and then the far more exciting M635CSi of 1984.

By the time of the M3's announcement in September 1985, however, the Motorsport division had established a new series of model-names. From now on, there would simply be an M (for Motorsport) followed by the single number of the car's series designation. The M5 had initiated the system in 1984, and now M3 would be used to mean the Motorsport edition of the 3 Series.

THE M3 ENGINE

Both the M1 and the M635CSi had versions of the same twin-cam 3.5ltr four-valve six-cylinder engine which had originally been developed for the works racing coupés. The crucially important feature of this engine was its cylinder head, which not only made

a huge difference to the engine's power and torque outputs but was also known to be reliable. A four-valve cylinder head of essentially similar design was also in use for the four-cylinder Formula 2 racing engines which the Motorsport division was then building.

So when the idea arose in 1981 that the Motorsport division should investigate a high-performance variant of the forthcoming E30 3 Series, there was little doubt about which way engine design would go. However, there appear to have been two schools of thought at first. Some Motorsport people thought that the four-valve six should be dropped into the E30 bodyshell to create the new car. Others disliked the idea, arguing that its weight would compromise the car's handling characteristics and that it would be simply too fast: BMW did not need all that power to make the proposed high-performance E30 faster than any likely competitors. They certainly had a point: the big six gave 286bhp in the M635CSi and was developed to give 315bhp in the M5.

The second school of thought favoured a four-cylinder engine, which would be lighter and would therefore not upset the car's handling balance. The four-cylinder would also be cheaper to build, and its use would aid model differentiation because the four-valve six would then be exclusive to the larger and more expensive Motorsport cars. In the end, the supporters of the four-cylinder engine won the day, although BMW certainly did build at least one prototype car with the Motorsport 3.5ltr four-valve six in an E30 bodyshell.

The first prototype of the four-cylinder engine which would eventually power the M3 was put together over the summer of 1981, under the supervision of Paul Rosche, the man behind all BMW's four-valve engines of the time. It was not a version of the Formula 2 four-cylinder engine, which was

M3 (1986–89)

Layout
Two-door saloon; cabriolet

Engine

Cylinders	Four
Bore × stroke	93.4mm × 84mm
Capacity	2302cc
Timing	Chain-driven ohc
Compression ratio	10.5:1
Fuel injection	Bosch Motronic ML engine management system
Max. power	200bhp at 6750rpm (non-cat); 195bhp at 6750rpm (cat)
Max. torque	177lb/ft at 4750rpm (non-cat); 170lb/ft at 4750rpm (cat)

Transmission

Gearbox	Five-speed close-ratio	
Ratios	Normal	US models
First	3.72:1	3.764:1
Second	2.40:1	2.40:1
Third	1.77:1	1.77.1
Fourth	1.26:1	1.26:1
Fifth	1.00:1	1.00:1
Final drive	3.25:1	4.1:1

Suspension and Steering

Front	Independent suspension with MacPherson struts, coil springs and anti-roll bar
Rear	Semi-trailing arm suspension with coil springs and anti-roll bar
Steering	Rack and pinion with 19.6:1 ratio
Wheels	7J × 15
Tyres	205/55 ZR 15

Brakes

Type	Servo-assisted with dual hydraulic circuit and ABS
Size	Front 284mm ventilated discs
	Rear 250mm solid discs

Dimensions

Track	Front 1,412mm/55.6in
	Rear 1,414m/56in
Wheelbase	2,562mm/100.9in
Overall length	4,345mm/171in
Overall width	1,680mm/66.1in
Overall height	1,370mm/53.9in
Unladen weight	1,285–1,415kg/2,833–3,120lb depending on specification

far too highly tuned and specialized for road car use. Instead, BMW took the block of one of its 2ltr four-cylinder engines and bored it out to the same 93.4mm as was used on the four-valve six. A specially-made crankshaft with the same 84mm stroke as the big six was added to give 2,302cc, and the four-valve cylinder head from a six-cylinder engine was cut and shut to suit the shorter four-cylinder block. The resulting engine allegedly gave excellent results first time around.

As a result, none of the engine's major details were changed during the ensuing development period, although a number of minor changes were made to ensure that the engine met BMW's strict reliability criteria. The project was headed by Werner Frowein, and persistent attention to detail produced a real gem of a motor, with 200bhp at 6750rpm and a generous 176lb/ft of torque at 4750rpm.

Yet only a few countries would ever get to see the M3 engine in this state of tune. The original brief had been to produce a high-performance engine without the exhaust catalyst demanded in the USA and in Japan, and BMW were prepared to accept that the car could not be sold in those markets. Then the West German government suddenly announced a series of incentives to encourage cleaner exhausts. Car makers were advised to offer catalytic converters from July 1985, and from that date cars so equipped would be exempted from road tax for a period (up to the end of 1987 for those with engines of more than 2 litres' capacity). Tax on unleaded fuel would also be reduced, tax on leaded fuel would be increased by a corresponding amount, and road tax would increase by 50 per cent for cars which could not run on unleaded fuel from the start of 1986.

These were powerful incentives, to manufacturers and the buying public alike, and the BMW engineers took heed. Besides, there were additional commercial advantages to consider: if the new M3 engine was available with a catalytic converter, it could be sold in the USA and in Japan as well as in the markets for which it had originally been intended. So a crash programme was initiated to develop a catalysed version of the engine. It speaks volumes for the engineers' dedication and perseverance that the cat-equipped engine entered production with 195bhp and 169lb/ft of torque – figures so close to those of the original engine that the car's performance was not noticeably affected.

GEARBOX AND RUNNING GEAR

The basic engine configuration seems to have been settled by the end of 1982, and early in the new year the Motorsport engineers started work on other areas of the car. The M3 project was entrusted to Thomas Ammerschläger, who had earned a formidable reputation working first on the Zakspeed Ford Capris and then on the original Audi Quattro.

To make the most of the new engine, BMW decided to use a sporting, close-ratio gearbox. They chose a five-speed type manufactured in Germany by Getrag, a racing-style gate with first gear out on a dog-leg and the other four gears in a conventional H-pattern. Other E30 five-speed gearboxes had fourth as the direct ratio and fifth as an overdrive, but the Getrag gave four closely-spaced gears with fifth as the direct ratio.

Fuel consumption was not going to be of too much concern to buyers of car like the M3, but BMW played for safety by giving it tall final-drive gearing: the engine was, after all, easily able to take it. Yet even that was not good enough for the US market, where the Getrag gearbox was replaced by the close-ratio Sport gearbox from the 325i. It appears that the importers believed their clients would react adversely to the unfamiliar gate pattern of the Getrag!

Durability was of the utmost importance to BMW, and so the clutch was given a special bonded lining. Driveability was also vital, and so the rear axle came as standard with a 25 per cent multi-plate limited-slip differential made by ZF. To the same ends, the steering was much quicker than on other E30 models, with a 19.6:1 ratio giving just 3.6 turns of the wheel from lock to lock as compared to 4.5 turns for a 325i. As demand from countries where right-hand drive was standard was expected to be relatively low, the decision was taken to offer the M3 only with left-hand drive, and no right-hand drive examples of this first-generation M3 would ever be made. The basic elements of the braking system came from the larger and heavier E28 5 Series cars, with the 284mm ventilated front discs of the 535i and 250mm solid discs at the rear. ABS was standard, of course, but was specially tuned to suit the sporting nature of the car.

The E30's suspension was already good, but it was a careful compromise which gave good ride comfort and good handling, without being biased towards one at the expense of the other. For the M3, the Motorsport engineers wanted to tilt the balance to improve the car's handling. Therefore, thicker anti-roll bars were specified, the front one having new pivot points outside the spring strut, and twin-tube Boge gas dampers were fitted all round. At the front, the strut geometry was altered, while changes at the rear involved stiffer springs and a change in the angle of the rear trailing arms to 15 degrees. Larger wheel bearings were fitted by the simple expedient of using stub axles from the E28 5 Series, and with these came hubs with five-stud wheel fixings. This meant that the M3 would always

The heart of the M3 was its 2.3ltr sixteen-valve engine. Onlookers were left in no doubt about its provenance, whether they were on the right-hand side . . .

. . . or the left.

Few people realized that the M3 had a differently-raked rear window and a higher boot lid than the standard E30 saloons. Both can be seen in this view of an early car.

Seen directly from behind, the M3 did not immediately attract attention as a high-performance car; spoilers were, after all, fashionable accessories in the 1980s.

An M3 was designed to be used as an everyday road car. This head-on view of an early car shows the standard fog lamps in the front air dam.

have wheels different from those on the other E30s, whose wheels were attached by four studs each. Those chosen for the first production cars were multi-spoke alloy types with 7in rims made by BBS, but some later examples would use different wheels, and the racing M3s used even wider rims.

THE BODY

Right from the start, there was no doubt that the two-door bodyshell would be chosen as the basis of the M3 because it was lighter than the four-door type and looked more sporting. Yet as the car took shape, so that bodyshell began to differ more and more from the standard production E30 styling – so much so, in fact, that of the major panels only the bonnet was shared with the standard production saloons.

The styling seems to have caused some headaches at BMW, and one story has it that the production design was delayed when senior management began to worry

that it was too aggressive. The differences also went way beyond the styling, affecting some ares of the structure itself. Even the fuel tank was different, because BMW thought the standard 55ltr (14.5gal) type would give insufficient range for a car which drank fuel at a rate which rarely bettered 20mpg. So the M3 had a 70ltr (18.5gal) tank.

The main reason why the M3 ended up looking so different from the standard E30s was that BMW had decided to take it racing. The bodyshell had to be fundamentally altered to allow a rollcage to be fitted (though this was not, of course, fitted to cars sold for road use). Wide wheels would be necessary for racing, and so the wings had to be flared to cover them. Aerodynamics would play an important part at high speeds on the race tracks, and so the car was equipped with front and rear spoilers. Its profile was also subtly changed by raising the line of the boot lid, and the rake of the rear window was altered to direct the airflow more positively towards the rear spoiler. Side sills were also re-shaped to

Although broadly similar to that of other E30s, the M3 driving environment had some special touches. Visible here are the three-spoke Motorsport wheel (with the Motorsport colours on the bottom of the centre spoke) and the Motorsport emblem between the two main dials. Note also the gearshift pattern on the gear knob: these cars had a dog's leg first gear.

improve airflow management, and the end result was an improvement in the Cd figure to 0.33 from the 0.36 of the standard car. For such a boxy shape, this was a remarkable achievement.

Although all four special wing panels were made of steel, tough SMC plastic was used for the other new panels. These were the front bumper and spoiler, the side sills, the rear bumper, the boot lid and the rear spoiler. The changed rake of the rear window of course meant that this was also a different shape from the type used on other E30s, and the need for maximum body rigidity in support of the improved handling meant that both this and the windscreen were bonded to the body rather than rubber-glazed in the traditional way.

INTERIOR AND EQUIPMENT

The designers fitted out the M3's interior in appropriate style for a high-performance sports saloon. That meant sombre upholstery materials, with the E30's optional Recaro

The M3 driver was provided with special sports seats in front . . .

. . . while the rear seat was shaped to accommodate just two passengers.

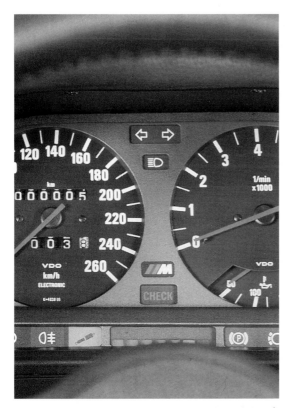

The Motorsport division's M logo was discreetly added between the main dials of the M3's instrument panel.

sports seats fitted as standard and a special rear seat contoured to take just two people. The dashboard was dominated by a three-spoke Motorsport steering wheel, and the instruments included a special 260km/h speedometer (160mph for countries which calculated in miles), an 8000rpm rev counter, an oil temperature gauge and a small Motorsport logo between the main dials.

Tinted windows and electrically-adjusted door mirrors were standard equipment, but other convenience aids were optional because the M3 was presented as a competition machine without fripperies. Thus air conditioning, electric windows, an electric sunroof, an on-board computer, leather seats and various in-car entertainment systems were all extra-cost options. Outside the car, so was a headlamp wash-wipe.

PRODUCTION

A pre-production prototype of the M3 was displayed on the BMW stand at the Frankfurt Motor Show in September 1985, but full production did not begin until September 1986.

By that stage, the rival Mercedes-Benz 190E 2.3-16 with its Cosworth-developed engine had been on sale for two years, and the arrival of the M3 raised the stakes in the battle for compact saloon sales between the two German companies.

Even though the M3 was a Motorsport model, its projected production volumes were too high to permit assembly at the division's new Garching factory, so the car was batch-produced at the main BMW factory in Munich. Yet it was never mass-produced in the same way as the other E30s; instead, special teams worked on sub-assemblies, most notably on the engine that was the heart of every M3.

The first production cars were built in September 1986, and the final M3 saloons in December 1990. The M3 cabriolet (*see* page 92) introduced in May 1988 lasted a few months longer, until July 1991. Yet there were relatively few production changes during the production life of the M3.

Production of engines without exhaust catalysts stopped in July 1989. That month, some special-edition models (*see* page 91) were the first to be equipped with a more powerful engine which developed 215bp with an exhaust catalyst, and this engine became standard for all markets in September. The new engine had its cam cover and air collector box painted in the Motorsport colours. Later on, the Boge-manufactured

EDC (Electronic Damper Control) became an option for the M3. This offered Sport, Normal and Comfort damper settings, with an automatic override of the Comfort setting in high-speed driving. No doubt the stiffer settings made a difference to the handling on the limit at high speeds, but few people have been able to detect the effects of changing the EDC settings in everyday driving!

THE EVOLUTION MODELS

As Chapter 9 reveals, BMW campaigned the M3 actively on the race-tracks in the late 1980s. Throughout that period, therefore, the company developed the car to keep it competitive, and FISA homologation regulations demanded that a minimum 500 of each major evolution of the original design had to be built. The road-going versions of the racing M3s were known as Evolution models and were sold as three limited editions. The first arrived in 1987, the second in 1988, and the third in 1989.

The first M3 Evolution was built between February and May 1987. There were 505 of these cars, which incorporated a number of modifications useful on the race-track but of no real value on the road. The engines in these cars were non-catalyst types, equipped with a different cylinder head and with other minor changes. Power, however, was quoted at the standard 200bhp. There was also a lightweight boot lid, but rather more obvious were changes to the front and rear spoilers designed to improve the car's aerodynamics at high speed. The front air dam had a small splitter extension, while the boot lid spoiler had a small lip underneath the main wing. Even more noticeable was that the front spoiler no longer carried fog lights, and that the apertures for these were filled by air ducts designed to direct cooling air onto the front brakes.

M3 (1989–91)

As for earlier M3, except as follows:

Layout   Two-door saloon (1989–90); cabriolet (1989–91)

Engine   Exhaust catalyst standard; 215bhp at 6750rpm and 170lb/ft at 4600rpm

---

How Fast Was the M3?

Figures taken by the leading motoring magazines of the day show the following.

	0-60mph	Standing ¼mile	Max speed	Source
M3 (non-cat, 1987)	6.8sec	N/A	143mph	*Car*
M3 (cat, 1987)	6.9sec	15.2sec	141mph	*Car & Driver*
Evolution II (1988)	6.6sec	15.2sec	148mph	*Autocar*
Sport Evolution (1990)	6.1sec	14.7sec	149mph	*Performance Car*
M3 Cabriolet (non-cat, 1989)	6.0sec	15.8sec	146mph	*Autocar*

The jutting front air dam and air ducts in place of the standard fog lamps make clear that this is one of the 1987 M3 Evolution models, of which just 505 were built.

M3 Evolution II (1988)

As for M3, except as follows:

Engine	11.1 compression ratio, 220bhp at 6750rpm and 181 lb/ft at 4750rpm
Final drive	3.15:1.
Wheels	7.5J × 16
Tyres	225/45 ZR 16

The second M3 Evolution, usually called the Evolution II model, was built between March and May 1988. There were 501 examples of this, which was much more distinctive than the earlier Evolution model. Special features started with a 220bhp engine, the extra power being achieved from a new camshaft and pistons, a raised compression ratio (to 11:1) and a re-chipped Motronic mangement system. The engine also had a lightened flywheel and a new air intake tube, and its cam cover and air collector were finished in white rather than the standard black, and carried the Motorsport coloured stripes. A taller final drive of 3.15:1 helped the maximum speed to go up from 146mph (235km/h) to 152mph (245km/h), but also explained why BMW claimed the same 0–62mph time of 6.7 seconds as was quoted for the standard M3.

The Evolution II had the same front and rear spoilers as the earlier Evolution model, but these were made of lightweight material. So were the bumper supports and boot lid, while additional weight was also saved in the rear screen and side windows. The total weight saving was around 10kg (22lb). Other distinguishing features were a windscreen with graduated tint, and wider tyres with a lower profile than standard. The wheels were 7.5 × 16 BBS multi-spoked alloys of the same design as the standard type, but

wider. Original-equipment tyres were Pirelli 225/45Z R 16s. Evolution II models came in just three colours, Macao Blue, Nogaro Silver and Misano Red, and all of them had a unique half-leather upholstery with checked cloth.

The third Evolution model is generally referred to as the Sport Evolution, but was originally called the Evolution III Sport. There were 600 of these cars, all built between December 1989 and March 1990. These were altogether more radical than the earlier Evolution models, their most notable feature being surely their new 2.5ltr engine. Developed to keep the cars competitive on the race-tracks, this had a big-bore version of the original block and a long-stroke crank to give a capacity of 2467cc. A new 282-degree camshaft, bigger inlet valves, sodium-cooled exhaust valves and oil sprayed on to the pistons from below to ensure adequate cooling were all part of the cocktail which promised 238bhp at 7000rpm and a further increase in maximum torque. The compression ratio, meanwhile, actually went down – to 10.2:1. With the 3.15:1 final drive seen on the Evolution II, maximum speed went up to 154mph (248km/h) and the 0–62mph sprint was reduced to 6.5 seconds.

The Sport Evolution was not easy to spot at a glance, because it looked much like the earlier Evolution II. Sharp eyes would have spotted fatter front wheelarches, designed to accept larger wheels on the racing cars, although the road cars had 7.5 × 16 BBS multi-spoke alloys once again, this time shod with Michelin MXX 225/45Z R 16 tyres. The front suspension was also 10mm (4in) lower than standard, and the spoilers were adjustable. Additional flaps under the front air dam and on top of the rear spoiler were attached by Allen screws and could be re-positioned to suit the downforce needed for maximum adhesion to a race track. Completely useless for normal road

The 1990 Sport Evolution had a new 2.5ltr engine, but was hard to distinguish from its predecessors.

use, they nevertheless attracted plenty of enthusiastic attention!

A lot of attention had also gone into the aerodynamics of these cars, and it showed in little details. A rubber strip ran between bonnet and wings, and there were further rubber inserts in the headlamp and front grille mountings. Even the vanes of the grille had supposedly been reprofiled, although it took very sharp eyes indeed to spot the difference there! As the new 2.5ltr engine was heavier than the earlier 2.3ltr type, work had also gone into weight-paring. Thus, the interior was devoid of map lights and roof grab handles, the rear and side window glasses were thinner, and the front and rear bumpers were lightened. Finally, the standard 70ltr (15.4gal)fuel tank had been replaced by the 62ltr (13.6gal) type from the 325i model.

M3 Sport Evolution III (1990)

As for M3, except as follows:

Engine

Cylinders	Four
Bore × stroke	95mm × 87mm
Capacity	2467cc
Timing	Chain-driven twin ohc
Compression ratio	10.2:1
Fuel injection	Bosch Motronic ML engine management system
Exhaust	Fitted with Lambda probe and three-way catalytic converter
Max. power	238bhp at 7000rpm
Max. torque	177lb/ft at 4750rpm
Final drive	3.15:1
Wheels	7.5J × 16
Tyres	225/45 ZR 16

By this stage, BMW was ready to exploit market interest in these special-edition cars to the hilt. Buyers of the Evolution III were rewarded with special interior features developed purely for their benefit and not for the drivers who campaigned these cars on the tracks. The three-spoke steering wheel now had a suede-covered rim, matched by suede on the handbrake grip and on the illuminated gear knob. There were special sports seats with wraparound wings at shoulder height, and with slots designed to receive racing harnesses (although few of them ever did). Upholstery and door trims were striped in a new pattern, the safety-belts had red webbing, and there was an M3 logo on the sill kick-plates. To complete the ensemble, each car carried a special plaque on the console which gave the model identity and year of manufacture – but not, as is sometimes suggested, the production number.

One that Got Away

The majority of M3s were two-door saloons, and a small number were cabriolets. However, BMW also considered building an M3 Touring version of the E30. The single prototype was claimed to be good for 150mph (241km/h). Production did not follow, probably because BMW considered there was no need for a third model alongside the existing saloon and cabriolet versions of the M3.

Evolution Models in the UK

Like the standard M3, the Evolution models were built only with left-hand drive, and this obviously limited their appeal to buyers in countries such as Britain where right-hand drive was the norm. The UK importers nevertheless did bring in small numbers of these cars. For the record, these were as follows:

Model	Total built	UK imports
Evolution (1987)	505	7
Evolution II (1988)	501	51
Sport Evolution (1989–90)	600	45

An Evolution air dam but with fog lamps? The dark centres to the multi-spoke wheels give the clue that this is one of the UK-market Roberto Ravaglia limited-edition cars.

This picture shows the Roberto Ravaglia limited-edition car much more clearly. Just visible is the twin-bladed rear spoiler, introduced earlier on the Evolution models.

The Evolution III was available only in two colours, Jet Black and Brilliant Red, and in each case there were contrasting bumper inserts. Red cars had black inserts, and black cars had red ones.

THE SPECIAL EDITIONS

BMW also exploited customer interest in special edition models by marketing two more limited-edition versions of the M3. The first appeared in 1988, and the second in 1989.

The first limited edition was designed to celebrate the M3's win in the 1988 European Touring Car Championship. Introduced in October 1988, it was known as the Europa Meister 88 Celebration edition. Just 150 were built, of which none came to the UK.

The car had the standard 195bhp catalyst-equipped engine, and was distinguished by full leather trim and by a dash plaque bearing the signature of M3 works driver Roberto Ravaglia.

The second limited edition was used to introduce the 215bhp catalyst-equipped engine in April 1989, some five months before this engine replaced the 195bhp catalyst and 200bhp non-catalyst types on standard production M3s. Once again, it traded on the M3's win in the 1988 touring car championship, and for all markets except the UK was known as the Johnny Cecotto edition, after the works driver. In the UK, however, it was called the Roberto Ravaglia edition.

The Cecotto and Ravaglia cars all had the extended front spoiler and double-blade rear spoiler already seen on the Evolution models.

The M3 cabriolet was introduced because of customer demand: BMW never had any intention of taking the car racing. The soft top fitted neatly, as on all the E30 cabriolets.

They had 7.5 × 16 BBS multi-spoke alloy wheels, distinguished by black-enamelled spokes, and were originally equipped with 225/45ZR16 Pirelli P-700-Z tyres. The Cecotto cars, of which there were 480, were all painted in Nogaro Silver, but the UK-market Ravaglia versions were painted Misano Red. All models had a special interior featuring half-leather seats with striped Motorsport cloth wearing faces. Silver-grey material was used for the headlining and sun visors, and on the dash panel and centre console, while an on-board computer was standard and the gear knob was illuminated. The finishing touch was a numbered plaque on the centre console, bearing the signature of the appropriate driver.

THE M3 CABRIOLET

It was customer demand which led to the introduction of the M3 cabriolet as a companion model to the standard saloon in May 1988. Although the car used the standard cabriolet bodyshell, it carried all the special M3 features such as the flared wings, BBS multi-spoke alloy wheels, and unique front spoiler. It did, however, lack the special boot lid and rear spoiler of the M3 saloon – because the cabriolet configuration would not allow them to be fitted. Instead, the M3 cabriolet had the boot lid and spoiler from the 325i model. Unlike lesser E30 cabriolets, it also had an electrically-operated soft top. All this added to the weight, and the car ended up a massive 160kg (353kg) heavier

The soft top was electrically operated on M3 cabriolets.

Top-down motoring with an M3 cabriolet was a very special experience. Note the standard rear head restraints.

than its saloon counterpart. Yet it was very nearly as fast as an M3 saloon.

Just 786 M3 cabriolets were built, production ending several months after that of the saloon, in July 1991. There were three main versions of the car, beginning with the 200bhp non-catalyst model, going on to the 195bhp catalyst type in October 1988, and ending with the 215bhp catalyst type in March 1990. Between June 1989 and February 1990 there was a gap in production, when no M3 cabriolets were built. All examples were assembled

M3 production

Annual production of the M3 models was as follows:

	Saloon	Cabriolet
1986	2397	
1987	6396	
1988	3426	130
1989	2541	180
1990	2424	176
1991		300
Total	17,184	786

Official imports to the UK began in 1987 and continued into 1992. The totals were as follows:

	Saloon	Cabriolet
1987	55	
1988	58	
1989	62	19
1990	36	13
1991	25	1
1992	21	
Total	257	33

M3 identification: VINs

Note: The VINs quoted here are for first and last cars only. The limited production nature of the M3 means that some cars within these ranges were not M3 models.

European non-catalyst models, October 1986 – July 1989
0842001 – 0845000
2190001 – 2192224
AE31000 – AE31242

European catalyst models, October 1986 – May 1989
1891001 – 1894694
AE40000 – AE40899

US catalyst models, December 1986 – December 1990
2195061 – 2198685
AE33000 – AE34628

Evolution models, February – May 1987
2190005 – 2190787

Evolution II models, March – May 1988
Individual chassis numbers

Europa Meister 88 Celebration models, October – November 1988
Chassis numbers not known

Cecotto and Ravaglia models, April – July 1989
Chassis numbers not known

215bhp models, September 1989 – December 1990
AE40900 – AE42418

Evolution III models, January – March 1990
AC79000 – AC79599

Cabriolet models, first batch, March 1988 – June 1989
2001552
2385001 – 2385042
EB85001 – EB 85093

Cabriolet models, second batch, October 1988 – June 1989
2001613
3559001 – 3559088
EB86000 – EB86085

Cabriolet models, third batch, March 1990 – June 1991
EB86086 – EB86561

at the Motorsport plant in Garching, as production numbers were small enough to be accommodated there.

Although there were no special editions of the M3 cabriolet, one car was built with the 220bhp engine from the Evolution II model. This unique example had chassis number EB 85020.

5 Third Generation – the E36 Models

With the third-generation 3 Series cars, BMW made a dramatic shift of emphasis. At the heart of the E21 and E30 ranges had been a two-door saloon model, but strong sales of the E30 four-door saloon variants suggested a new strategy. Thus the core model of the E36 range introduced in 1990 was not the traditional sporting two-door saloon but rather a family-oriented four-door model.

None of this prevented the E36 range from retaining all the sporting characteristics of its forebears, of course. What happened was that BMW developed a two-door model and called it a coupé, to add cachet and justify a higher showroom price. They then went on to expand the range even further, adding the expected Touring and soft-top cars (the latter now called 'convertible' by the factory), and supplementing these by a new entry-level two-door model called the Compact. To the expected range of four-cylinder petrol, six-cylinder petrol, and six-cylinder diesel engines, they went on to add a four-cylinder diesel as well. All this broadened the appeal of the 3 Series range and added to sales and to BMW's profits.

The E36 styling has worn well, and still looks elegant a decade after it was conceived.

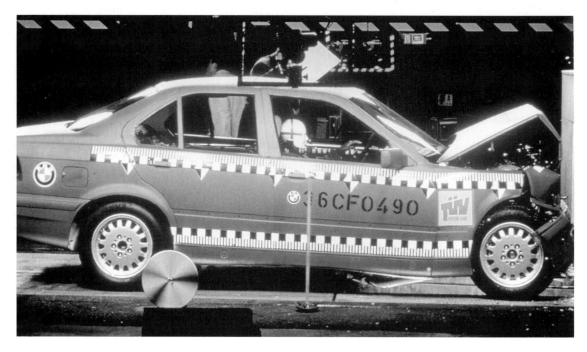

The third-generation 3 Series was engineered to meet the most stringent safety regulations. An example is seen here being crash-tested against a barrier to satisfy the German TüV authorities.

As always, alloy wheels made a world of difference to the car's appearance. This is a 1991 left-hand drive model. The chiselled 'spoiler' styling of the boot lid's trailing edge is evident here.

The E30 models set the pace in the small saloon market during the 1980s. This is a 323i model, with the six-cylinder 2.3ltr engine.

Estate versions of the E30 were also available, under the Touring name. Load capacity was limited, but the cars made stylish family holdalls.

Styled steel wheels made even the entry-level E21 316 look up-market.

The E36 third-generation cars were once again distinctively styled. Core model of the range was the four-door saloon, seen here in 1997 guise.

The M3 version of the E36 started life as a two-door coupé, but other body styles were added later.

The Compact version of the E36 may have been the entry-level model, but it could look extremely purposeful with the right cosmetic additions.

The red leather interior sets off this E36 convertible to perfection.

BMW introduced its own cabriolet body for the E30 in 1986, to replace the Baur targa-top conversions.

There was never any pretence that the E36 M3 convertible was designed for racing, although its road performance was outstanding. It was really a well-equipped high-performance open car which appealed to wealthy (and fortunate) buyers.

Stylish once again, the E36 Touring was a practical family machine which also offered high performance when equipped with one of the six-cylinder engines.

Most exciting of the E30s was undoubtedly the M3, introduced primarily so that BMW could go Touring Car racing.

The coupé version of the fourth-generation E46 car carried on the style established by its E36 predecessors.

Even the cheaper versions of the E46 fourth-generation models were astonishingly attractive. This is a 318i saloon.

An E46 coupé is pictured here at speed. Note the absence of badges from this pre-production car, pictured in Germany.

Interior styling had become a strength by the time of the E36s and E46s. This is the attractive and inviting driving compartment of an E46 coupé.

Occupant safety was an important consideration for all the 3 Series, but never more so than when the E46 was being designed. This ghosted view of a coupé shows the variety of airbags available – though not all of them were standard.

The expected convertible version of the E46 was announced during 1999.

The M3 version of the E46 was shown at the 1999 Frankfurt Motor show. It was expected to go on sale in 2000, possibly in the summer.

The E30 M3 was available in a limited variety of colours, and this red suited the car perfectly.

316i (1990–98)

Layout
Four-door saloon; two-door coupé (1992–98); Compact (1994–98)

Engine
Cylinders	Four
Bore × stroke	84mm × 72mm
Capacity	1596cc
Timing	Belt-driven ohc
Compression ratio	9.0:1
Fuel injection	Bosch Motronic engine management system
Exhaust	Fitted with Lambda probe and three-way catalytic converter
Max. power	100bhp at 5000rpm; 102bhp at 5500rpm (1993–98)
Max. torque	102lb/ft at 4250rpm; 110lb/ft at 3900rpm (1993–98)

Transmission
Gearbox	Five-speed close-ratio	
Ratios	Normal	Four-speed overdrive automatic
First	4.23:1	2.40:1
Second	2.52:1	1.47:1
Third	1.77:1	1.00.1
Fourth	1.26:1	0.72:1
Fifth	1.00:1	
Final drive	3.45:1	4.45:1

Suspension and Steering
Front	Independent suspension with MacPherson struts, coil springs and anti-roll bar
Rear	Multi-link suspension with coil springs and anti-roll bar; coupé models have 'Z-axle' with semi-trailing arms and separate springs and dampers
Steering	Rack and pinion with 16.8:1 ratio; power assistance standard form June 1992
Wheels	6J × 15 (7J × 15 on coupé)
Tyres	185/65 HR 15 (205/60 VR 15 on coupé)

Brakes
Type	Servo-assisted with dual hydraulic circuit; ABS optional 1990–91 and standard from November 1991
Size	Front 286mm discs
	Rear 228.6mm drums; 280mm rear discs, with ABS 1990–91

Dimensions
Track	Front 1,418mm/55.8in
	Rear 1,431m/56.3in (1,423mm/56in on Compact models)
Wheelbase	2,700mm/106.3in
Overall length	4,433mm/174.5in (4,210mm/165.7in on Compact models)
Overall width	1,698mm/66.8in
Overall height	1,393mm/54.8in
Unladen weight	1,210–1,423kg/2,667–2,756lb, depending on specification

Work had begun on the E36 range during the 1980s, while the E30 models were at the peak of their success. Yet no-one at BMW was blind to the failings of these second-generation 3 Series models. Fundamentally, they were too small, and their upright styling was too conservative and had started to look dated. So development work was devoted towards the elimination of these shortcomings, and towards improvements in other areas. Thus, the cars had to become even more fuel efficient as well as faster, to be safer as well as offer better handling, and they needed to be cheaper to run through less need for servicing. In addition, BMW had embraced the idea of the recyclable car, and the E36 was designed to be 80 per cent recyclable at the end of its life.

The question of size was addressed right from the beginning, and the E36 was 110mm (4.33in) longer than the E30 it replaced, 50mm (1.96in) wider and 10mm (0.4in) taller. Most significant, however, was that the wheelbase was a full 127mm (5in) longer than before. Yet only 38mm (1.5in) of this was devoted to increasing legroom for the rear seat passengers – and, frankly, it was not enough. BMW had clearly seen the longer wheelbase primarily as a means to improving ride comfort. Additional space in the longer car was also used up by an increase in the capacity of the boot.

The bodyshell designers also aimed to provide better crash protection, and in this they succeeded extremely well. Much stiffer than the E30 type, the four-door E36 bodyshell comfortably exceeded the 1990 US Federal requirements, which were then the toughest in the world. Oddly, however, the traditional BMW front-hinged bonnet with its excellent crash-protection properties had been replaced by a conventional rear-hinged type. Better corrosion protection had been among the design criteria as

318i (1990–98)

Layout
Four-door saloon; convertible (1993 on); Touring (1995 on)

Engine

Cylinders	Four
Bore × stroke	84mm × 81mm
Capacity	1796cc
Timing	Belt-driven ohc
Compression ratio	8.8:1
Fuel injection	Bosch Motronic engine management system
Exhaust	Fitted with Lambda probe and three-way catalytic converter
Max. power	113bhp at 5500rpm; 115bhp at 5500rpm (1993–98)
Max. torque	117lb/ft at 4250rpm; 124lb/ft at 3900rpm (1993–98)

Transmission

Gearbox	As for 316i

Suspension and Steering
As for 316i, but power-assisted steering always standard

Brakes
As for 316i

Dimensions
As for 316i, except unladen weight 1,225–1,265kg/2,700–2,789lb, depending on specification

well, and the E36 shell had an increased number of panels which were zinc-coated on both sides. It also incorporated plastics in its construction, most visibly in the fluted sill panels whose dark grey colour helped to slim the side elevation.

Better aerodynamics had also been on the agenda, and these were reflected in

The earliest cars had dark grey plastic sills and aprons, which did nothing for what was otherwise a sleek design, and sports-styled plastic wheel trims. This is an early 316i, the entry-level model.

On this later car – a 1994 318tds – note how the grey areas have been reduced to improve the car's looks. The glassed-over headlamps were a first on a BMW.

the styling. With this third-generation car, BMW broke for good with the upright design of the E21s and E39s, using a much sleeker shape with more rounded contours. The aerodynamic aids were also more skilfully integrated into the design, and the air dam under the front bumper and the aerofoil shape of the boot lid's trailing edge did not look like the afterthoughts they had been on earlier models.

A steeply-raked windscreen, glassed-over headlamps and side glass which was very

320i (1990–96)

Layout
Four-door saloon; coupé (1992 on); cabriolet (1993 on); Touring (1995 on)

Engine

Cylinders	Six
Bore × stroke	80mm × 66mm
Capacity	1991cc
Valves	Four per cylinder
Timing	Belt-driven ohc; VANOS variable valve timing from September 1992
Compression ratio	11.0:1
Fuel injection	Bosch Motronic M1.7 engine management system
Exhaust	Fitted with Lambda probe and three-way catalytic convertoer
Max. power	150bhp at 5900rpm
Max. torque	140lb/ft at 4700rpm

Transmission

Gearbox	Five-speed close-ratio	
Ratios	Normal	Five-speed overdrive automatic
First	4.23:1	3.67:1
Second	2.52:1	2.00:1
Third	1.77:1	1.41.1
Fourth	1.26:1	1.00:1
Fifth	1.00:1	0.74:1
Final drive	3.45:1	4.45:1

Suspension and Steering
As for 316i, except for 6.5J × 15 wheels (saloon) or 7J × 15 wheels (coupé), both with 205/60 VR 15 tyres. Power steering standard

Brakes
As for 316i, but ventilated front discs, ABS and 280mm rear disc brakes always standard

Dimensions

Track	Front 1,408mm/55.4in
	Rear 1,421mm/55.9in.
Wheelbase	2,700mm/106.3in
Overall length	4,433mm/174.5in
Overall width	1,698mm/66.8in (saloon) or 1,710mm/67.3in (coupé)
Overall height	1,393mm/54.8in (saloon) or 1,366mm/53.8in (coupé)
Unladen weight	1,335–1,370kg/2,943–3,020lb, depending on specification

nearly flush-fitting were only the more obvious details. Even the twin-kidney grille was smaller than before, neatly incorporated in a sloping front panel, and a close look revealed not only airflow deflectors ahead of all four wheels but also underbody panels to smooth out the airflow beneath the car. The end result was a reduction in aerodyanmic drag compared to the E30 models, with Cd figures ranging from 0.29 for the narrow-tyred 316i up to 0.32 for the fatter-tyred six-cylinder cars.

Suspension design at the front followed previous practice in its use of MacPherson stuts, and all models came with an anti-roll bar. However, the design had been further refined, and while the four-cylinder cars used a combined strut damper and coil spring, the springs and dampers were separately mounted on six-cylinder derivatives. At the rear, the suspension still used trailing arms, with an anti-roll bar on the more powerful cars, but its design was very different from what had gone before. The E36 rear suspension was a further development of the so-called 'Z-axle' designed by BMW

Technik for the Z1 two-seater, modified to give more spring travel and bring roll comfort up to the levels expected in a saloon. BMW called it the central-arm rear axle, and it incorporated mounting bushes which were flexible enough to provide a degree of active steering.

Twin-tube gas dampers were used all round, again to improve ride comfort, and BMW finally addressed the problem of slow steering. Although cheaper models were sold in Germany with a very slow manual steering system, the power-assisted rack and pinion steering which was standard on

---

325i (1990–95)

Layout
Four-door saloon; coupé (1992 on); convertible (1993 on)

Engine
Cylinders	Six
Bore × stroke	84mm × 75mm
Capacity	2494cc
Valves	Four per cylinder
Timing	Belt-driven single ohc; VANOS variable valve timing from September 1992
Compression ratio	10.5:1
Fuel injection	Bosch Motronic M1.7 engine management system
Exhaust	Fitted with Lambda probe and three-way catalytic converter
Max. power	192bhp at 5900rpm
Max. torque	177lb/ft at 4200rpm

Transmission
Five-speed close-ratio manual (ratios as for 316i) with 3.15:1 final drive, or five-speed overdrive automatic (ratios as for 320i) with 3.15:1 final drive

Suspension and Steering
As for 316i, except 7J × 15 wheels with 205/60 VR 15 tyres. Power steering standard

Brakes:
As for 316i, but ventilated front discs, ABS and rear disc brakes always standard

Dimensions
As for 320i; cabriolet dimensions as for coupé except overall height (open) 1,348mm/53in; wheelbase of cabriolet 2,696mm/106.1in; unladen weight 1,360–1,505kg/2,998–3,318lb, depending on specification

the more expensive cars and optional elsewhere was much quicker than before.

As for wheel sizes, once again BMW had gone up an inch. The E21s had 13in wheels as standard, the E30s went up to 14in, and all models of the E36 range came with 15in wheels as standard. Steel wheels were equipped with flush-fitting silver-grey plastic trims which gave a quite convincing impression of alloy wheels, and the real thing was of course available at extra cost. These bigger wheels allowed for further enlarged brakes, an all-disc system on the six-cylinder cars and a disc/drum type on

Seen in a two-door model are the inertia-reel seat belts of the E36. BMW believed that straps in the centre of the seat rather than at the outboard edges provided improved occupant retention.

The E36 interior was always neatly styled, and careful use of colour removed the sombre character associated with earlier 3 Series interiors. The upper picture shows the dashboard of a 1997 model, and the lower shows the interior of a four-door saloon of the same vintage.

the four-cylinders. However, if the optional ABS was ordered on a four-cylinder E36, rear discs came with it. It was only later that BMW developed a satisfactory ABS system for use with the disc/drum system.

Interior design was re-thought, and the dashboard featured softer curves than its predecessors. With a centre section still angled towards the driver, it had a distinctive large air vent in the centre. There was provision for both driver's and passenger's airbags, and the requirement for the latter had led to one of BMW's less successful pieces of design – a rather flimsy plastic glove-box lid which quickly earned criticism from press and public alike. Redesigned seats were upholstered in woven cloth; leather was optional for the six-cylinder models, and there was also a sports front seat option. The standard steering wheel was a four-spoke design; an airbag-equipped version was optional (and standard in some markets), and there was of course the usual three-spoke sports wheel option as well.

The interior was one area of the original design which did not work well. Early customers complained of poor-quality plastic components, of rattles and squeaks from the dashboard, of door trims which fell off, and of sundry other problems such as leaking sunroofs and inadequate door seals. BMW managed to keep most of the problems out of the public eye, but responded very rapidly and by the late spring of 1991 were rushing through a series of changes. The woven cloth upholstery was changed for a more expensive-looking velour, which was also applied to the door trims. Cloth was added to the bulkhead at the front of the boot on all models, and to the underside of the boot lid on six-cylinder cars. And the cheap-looking glovebox lid, originally black, was finished to match the colour of the upholstery. Improved quality control on the production line dealt with the other problems at the same time.

THE ENGINES

Over the years, the E36 range was host to a much wider variety of engines than had been seen in the earlier 3 Series ranges. There were three families of petrol four-cylinder: the M40, M42 and M44. Two families of six-cylinder were used, the M52 replacing the earlier M50 in the mid-1990s. All these were of course fuel-injected and used increasingly sophisticated management systems manufactured by Bosch. On the diesel side, the M51 turbocharged six-cylinder was later joined by an M41 four-cylinder engine.

The engines in the first E36 models belonged to just two families, however, these being the M40 four-cylinders and the M50

six-cylinders. The M40 fours were carried over from the E30 models, although both the 1596cc engine in the 316i and the 1796cc type in the 318i had been substantially developed in detail. Among the more important changes were reworked cylinder heads which gave better gas flow, and shorter pistons which were lighter and made for smoother running. The latest Bosch Motronic M1.7 engine management system was used on both engines, too. Many people failed to appreciate the changes which had been made, largely because the quoted power outputs of 100bhp and 113bhp respectively were identical to those of the earlier M40 engines.

The M50 six-cylinder engines were new to the 3 Series, although they had been introduced a few months earlier in 1990 for the E34 5 Series cars. Both the 150bhp, 1991cc type in the 320i and the 192bhp, 2494cc type in the 325i had four valves per cylinder and, in common with BMW's latest thinking, chain drives for their twin overhead camshafts. Their engine management systems were Bosch DME 3.1 types, which brought fully-sequential fuel injection and a single ignition coil for each cylinder. Weight was saved by the use of thermoplastic inlet manifolds, and styled plastic engine covers were used in order to present an attractive underbonnet appearance. This was a first for BMW, and a practice which they would follow on every subsequent new engine. The 320i version of the E36 was good for 133mph (214km/h), while the top-model 325i would reach 145mph (233km/h).

The M50 sixes were initially built with conventional valve-gear, but from September 1992 they took on BMW's new VANOS system, which had been available earlier only on the Motorsport-developed engines. VANOS was a system which varied the valve timing by hydraulically moving the inlet

The first diesel engine to appear in the E36 range was the 2.5ltr six-cylinder. It is seen here in 115bhp 325td guise; later, there would also be an intercooled version with 143bhp in the 325tds.

camshaft forwards or backwards in its housing. The main benefits were that valve timing could be optimized at all engine speeds, thus giving both good bottom-end torque and good top-end power without compromise to either.

Meanwhile, 1991 saw the introduction of the first diesel model in the range, using the latest 2498cc six-cylinder M51 turbodiesel to give the 325td 121mph (195km/h) performance. This engine had been developed from the earlier M21 six-cylinder diesel, but had been redesigned specifically as a turbocharged engine, with a longer stroke and a chain-driven camshaft. There never would be a naturally-aspirated version,

The original four-valve 1.8ltr engine was uprated to 1.9ltr in the 318iS and 318ti.

325td (1991–98)

Layout
Four-door saloon

Engine

Cylinders	Six
Bore × stroke	80mm × 82.5mm
Capacity	2498cc
Timing	Belt-driven single ohc
Compression ratio	22.0:1
Fuel injection	Bosch DDE engine management system
Turbocharger	Garrett exhaust-driven
Exhaust	Fitted with Lambda probe and three-way catalytic converter
Max. power	115bhp at 4800rpm
Max. torque	160lb/ft at 1900rpm

Transmission

Gearbox	Five-speed close-ratio manual	
Ratios	Normal	four-speed overdrive automatic
First	5.09:1	2.66:1
Second	2.80:1	1.62:1
Third	1.76:1	1.00:1
Fourth	1.25:1	0.72:1
Fifth	1.00:1	
Final Drive	2.65:1	3.23:1

Suspension and Steering
As for 325i, except 6J × 15 wheels with 185/65 HR 15 tyres

Dimensions
As for 316i, except unladen weight 1,335–1370kg/2,943–3020lb, depending on specification

---

but a more powerful edition equipped with an intercooler was introduced in 1993 for the 130mph (209km/h) 325tds model.

Next on the agenda was a more powerful four-cylinder for the 318iS model in 1992. This had the same swept volume and twin-overhead camshaft configuration as the four-valve M42 type in the E30 318iS, but it had been redeveloped with a new variable intake manifold to give a better spread of torque; once again, the quoted power output of 140bhp (just 4bhp more than the E30 318iS) did not do justice to the amount of work which had gone into the engine. This engine was replaced in the 318iS in

1995 by the 1895cc M44 four-cylinder, which had first put in an appearance during 1994 in a special high-performance version of the Compact known as the 318ti and would later also be used in the Z3 roadster.

During 1994, BMW also introduced a completely new type of engine to the E36 range, in the shape of a four-cylinder turbocharged diesel. The M41 engine was, broadly speaking, a four-cylinder edition of the existing M51 six-cylinder turbodiesel, and shared the bigger engine's bore and stroke dimensions. While it gave excellent fuel economy, its 90bhp were nevertheless

325tds (1993–98)

As for 325td, except:

Layout
As for 325td, but with the addition of Touring from 1994

Engine
Induction system equipped with intercooler; exhaust equipped with oxidating catalytic converter; 143bhp at 4800rpm and 192lb/ft at 2200rpm

Transmission

Gearbox	Five-speed close-ratio manual	
Ratios	Normal	five-speed overdrive automatic
First	5.09:1	3.67:1
Second	2.80:1	2.00:1
Third	1.76:1	1.41:1
Fourth	1.25:1	1.00:1
Fifth	1.00:1	0.74:1
Final Drive	2.56:1	2.56:1

Wheels and Tyres
6.5J × 15 wheels with 205/60 R 15 tyres

Unladen weight
1,350–1,385kg/2,976–3,053lb, depending on specification

There was no doubting the refinement of the four-cylinder diesel, but its performance was a little underwhelming for a BMW. BMW took the usual care over its presentation in the engine bay.

For the E36 range, BMW developed its first four-cylinder diesel engine and badged the cars as 318tds models.

only barely adequate, and BMW did not pursue this engine after the E46 models replaced the E36 types four years later.

The final new engines for the E36 models were a pair of M52 six-cylinders that arrived in 1996. Like the earlier M50s which they replaced, these were four-valve types with chain-driven twin overhead camshafts and VANOS variable valve timing, but they sported lightweight alloy cylinder blocks instead of the iron blocks of the earlier engines. The 193bhp 2793cc variant went into the 328i model that replaced the older 325i at the top of the range, while a 170bhp 2494cc type went into a new 323i model. The fact that its capacity was identical to that of the M50 in the superseded 325i only added to the confusion: BMW's explanation was that the 323i offered a 2.5ltr engine at the price of other manufacturers' 2.3ltr types. At the same time, the M50 engine of the 320i was updated with a new lightweight alloy block of the same design as the M52 types.

M52 Engine Problems

As introduced, the M52 six-cylinder engines had Nikasil coating of the cylinder bores. This was introduced to reduce friction and to protect the alloy cylinder block from wear, and was chosen over conventional steel liners as a way of saving weight. BMW had used the Nikasil coating process earlier, in its 1992 V8 engines for the 5, 7 and 8 Series.

However, this coating was found to degrade under certain conditions (notably when excessive sulphur was present in the petrol used). A number of engines thus affected were replaced under warranty by BMW, and from mid-1997 the M52 engines were re-engineered to take conventional steel cylinder liners.

The 1994 318iS Class 2

BMW buyers in Germany were treated to a unique 'homologation special' version of the 318iS from April 1994. The works-supported Super Touring racers needed additional spoilers and other changes that year in order to remain competitive, and the regulations demanded a minimum of 2500 production cars with these modifications. So the 318iS Class 2 was introduced, named after the class in which the works racers were competing.

The 318iS Class 2 had the four-door saloon bodyshell, and the four-valve engine which was then still unique to the 318iS coupé. It featured an M3-style front bumper moulding with blanked-off air intake, extra driving lamps and a rubber lip along the lower edge. At the rear were a combined bumper and apron, and a discreet two-tier boot lid spoiler. The sills also carried moulded extensions.

Bodyside rubbing strips were fitted, with Motorsport International badges let into them at the leading edge of each front door. Standard wheels were five-spoke alloys with 235/40 ZR 17 tyres, and the interior came with a three-spoke airbag steering wheel and bucket front seats with adjustable thigh supports. The wearing surfaces of the seats were trimmed with a striking diagonal-pattern fabric.

The 1994 318iS Class 2 was the only four-door model with the four-valve 1.8ltr engine.

GEARBOXES

During the 1980s, overdrive manual gear-boxes had been the core transmissions of the E30 range, but for the 1990s BMW took a different approach. The right levels of fuel economy were now achievable through more sophsticated engine management systems, and the new manual gearboxes introduced for the E36 models focussed instead on driving enjoyment. Thus, they had five closely-spaced ratios to give a sporting feel, with fifth gear being a direct-drive ratio. Three different gear-sets were available, one suiting the four-cylinder diesel engine, a second suiting the two six-cylinder diesels, and a third for all other models. (The M3, however, had its own special set of ratios, as the next chapter shows.) At the beginning of production, there were quality-control problems here, just as there had been with the interior fittings of the E36, and many cars were given new gearboxes under warranty.

Automatic transmissions, however, still needed overdrive top gears, so the existing four-speed gearbox was made available as an option for the four-cylinder E36 models and, with a different gear set, for the six-cylinder 325td. All the other six-cylinder models, however, including the 325tds, had a new five-speed automatic with four more closely-spaced ratios and an overdrive top gear. Once again, this new transmission was made by ZF in Germany. It featured electro-hydraulic control, with a choice of three shift modes. These were Sport, for maximum acceleration, Economy, for normal everyday driving, and Winter, designed to reduce wheelspin. In the Sport mode, the overdrive top gear was locked out, unless there was a danger of overspeeding the engine.

VARIATIONS ON A THEME

As already noted, the four-door E36 saloon introduced in 1990 was only the core model of the range. While BMW prepared its companions, production of the low-volume E30 variants continued, and the cabriolets and Touring estates remained available alongside the new E36 saloon.

The first E36 variant to appear was the Coupé, announced in January 1992. Although this was very recognizably related to the existing saloon, it was actually a much more different car than it appeared at first sight. Not only did it have just two doors, but it also had a redesigned roofline which made it some 30mm (1.2in) lower overall, more steeply raked front and rear screens, and lower bonnet and boot lines. There was also a slight difference in the width, of 10mm (0.4in), which reflected just how different the sheet metal really was. Tail light clusters, too, were unique.

Intended from the start as the sporty-looking variant – a rôle which it fulfilled admirably – the Coupé took a step back-wards as far as the rear seat passengers were concerned. The lower roofline and steeply-raked rear screen made space in the back very cramped, especially for tall people. However, the seats were designed to fold forwards to create a flat platform for luggage, and as a stylish two-seater touring car the Coupé made a lot more sense. Interesting features in its construction included automatic retraction of the drop-glasses to allow the doors to shut cleanly. It was also possible to order elec-tric operation of the rear quarter-windows, but these opened so little that there was hardly any point.

The Coupé body shell was not made avail-able with every engine in the range. There were no diesels, and nor was there a 318i. Instead of the latter came a special 318iS

With the four-door models now occupying centre stage, the two-door version of the car was designed as a stylish coupé.

model, available only in this two-door form and featuring a 140bhp twin-cam four-cylinder M42 engine which was not offered in any other E36 variant.

BMW's next new bodyshell was the convertible, and this time the standard English-language description replaced the cabriolet name which had been favoured for the E30 cars. Its bodyshell was quite logically based upon that of the two-door Coupé, although various underbody reinforcements made the wheelbase very slightly different. The Convertible appeared in 1993 as a 318i, 320i or 325i, the six-cylinder engines always having VANOS variable valve timing. When the 323i and 328i models were created by the introduction of the new M52 engines, the convertible nomenclature followed suit.

Even though the convertible bodyshell was based upon the Coupé, it had been developed and engineered separately from the beginning. Most important of the differences were extra reinforcements to preserve the rigidity of the roofless shell in everyday motoring, and additional work to ensure its crashworthiness. Thus, the windscreen frame was immensely strong – BMW claimed it would take the full weight of a 316i without buckling – so that it acted as a front rollover bar. Behind the seats, meanwhile, additional rollover protection bars popped up automatically if the car tilted past a certain point, in order to protect passengers in the rear seats. BMW claimed that the convertible not only surpassed the tough US Federal rollover requirements for open-top cars, but also met the even stiffer regulations which applied to saloons.

The convertible top of the E30 cabriolets had set a standard for other manufacturers, but BMW managed to improve on it with the

---

318iS (1992–95)

Layout
Two-door coupé; 2500 special-edition '318iS Class 2' models in 1994 with four-door saloon body

Engine
Cylinders	Four
Bore × stroke	84mm × 81mm
Capacity	1796cc
Valves	Four per cylinder
Timing	Chain-driven ohc
Compression ratio	10.0:1
Fuel injection	Bosch Motronic M1.7 engine management system
Exhaust	Fitted with Lambda probe and three-way catalytic converter
Max. power	140bhp at 6000rpm
Max. torque	129lb/ft at 4500rpm

Transmission
As for 316i

Suspension and Steering
Suspension	As for 318i
Wheels	7J × 15 wheels
Tyres	205/60 VR 15

Brakes
As for 318i, but ABS and rear disc brakes always standard

Dimensions
Track	Front 1,408mm/55.4in
	Rear 1,421m/55.9in
Wheelbase	2,700mm/106.3in
Overall length	4,433mm/174.5in
Overall width	1,710mm/67.3in
Overall height	1,366mm/53.8in
Unladen weight	1,265–1,300kg/2,789–2,866lb, depending on specification

---

soft top on the E36 convertibles. Sealing was more effective, the headlining reduced noise more efficiently and the rear window was more easily removable for repair. But what attracted the customers was the collection of convenience features which now came as standard. For a start, the soft top was electrically operated, and it had a twist-grip release on the windscreen which could be released by one hand. All four electrically-powered windows could be raised or lowered together by means of a single switch, and all four windows dropped automatically by 15mm (0.6in) to allow the soft top to close easily. This meant that the driver did not have to remember to lower the windows one by one before raising the soft top. Optional on all E36 convertibles were an air deflector which fitted across the rear seats and stored in the boot when not in use, and a hugely expensive aluminium hardtop, painted in the body colour.

From the coupé was developed the convertible – yet another extraordinarily attractive design from BMW. Those alloy wheels do the car no favours, though.

With the Compact models, introduced in 1994, BMW was tackling a new market. The plan was to build a competitor in the 'hot hatch' market and, rather than building a completely new car, the company had decided to develop a version of the E36 3 Series. To that end, a new three-door hatchback body was designed, with a truncated tail and rear seats which folded down in typical hatchback fashion. While the nose of the car was recognizably E36 3 Series, and the 106.3-inch wheelbase of the saloons was retained, most of the rest of the shell was new. Whether it was also pretty is a matter for debate: to eyes used to the beautifully-balanced three-box saloon and coupé shapes, the two-box Compact looked as if it had been involved in a rear-end shunt.

316i Compact (1998–99)

As for earlier 316i, but fitted with 1895cc four-valve engine from the 1995–98 318iS, detuned to give 105bhp and 122lb/ft.

The truncated rear end demanded some special engineering solutions. In order to provide a flat floor in the boot, the standard E36 central-arm suspension was replaced by the trailing-arm set-up from the old E30 models. The space-saver spare wheel was also relocated under the boot floor. Other modifications were designed to maintain the collision resistance properties of the shorter rear end. Thus, while reinforcement ensured that the car would easily meet the US 30mph rear-end impact requirement, the rear seat belt upper mountings were relocated outboard, as there was no bulkhead to mount them to. The tailgate, which reached down almost to bumper level to give a low loading sill, came with a wash-wipe system as standard. However, the demister element in its glass did not contain the radio aerial, as on other E36 models. Instead, a mast aerial was fitted to the rear wing.

Strangely, BMW had also felt it necessary to redesign the facia, which now had twin central air vents similar to those of the bigger 5 Series and 7 Series cars, rather than the large angled vent of the saloons.

318td and 318tds (1994–98)

Layout
318td as Compact only; 318tds as four-door saloon and Touring

Engine
Cylinders	Four
Bore × stroke	80mm × 82.8mm
Capacity	1665cc
Timing	Chain-driven ohc
Compression ratio	22.0:1
Fuel injection	Bosch DDE engine management system
Exhaust	Fitted with Lambda probe and three-way catalytic convertoer
Max. power	90bhp at 4400rpm
Max. torque	140lb/ft at 2000rpm

Transmission
Gearbox	Five-speed close-ratio manual
Ratios	
First	5.43:1
Second	2.95:1
Third	1.81:1
Fourth	1.26:1
Fifth	1.00:1
Final drive	2.65:1

Suspension and Steering
As for 316i, but power-assisted steering and ABS with drum rear brakes always standard

Brakes
As for 316i, but ABS with drum rear brakes always standard

Dimensions
As for 316i, except unladen weight 1,195kg/2,634lb (Compact); 1,265kg/2,789lb (four-door saloon)

318ti (1994 on)

All details as for 316i Compact, except:

Layout Compact
Engine As for 318iS initially; new engine as for later 318iS from 1995
Brakes Ventilated front discs

The 323ti introduced six-cylinder power to the Compact range.

However, the basic design was instantly recognizsable as BMW, and the rest of the interior reflected existing 3 Series practice. The trick had been to make the car more cheaply in order to sell it more cheaply, to retain some kind of differentiation between the Compact and the more expensive 'full-size' models, and yet not to lose the traditional BMW quality feel. BMW had pulled it off rather well.

The hatchback market was one for four-cylinder engines, and BMW conformed by not making any six-cylinder Compact available – at least, not in the beginning. There were 316i and 318tds versions, and at the top of the Compact range came a 318ti, which had the 140bhp 1.8ltr engine from the 318iS. Later, it followed the 318iS in switching to a similarly-powered 1.9ltr type. The letters 'ti' were deliberately chosen to give the car something of a new image; they recalled the high-performance 'ti' BMWs of the 1960s, and they also hinted at the GTi

The Compact looked like a standard 3 Series from the front, but the truncated tail made for a very different appearance from the side or the rear. With this car, which was priced as an entry-level 3 Series, BMW planned to attract customers away from 'hot hatches'.

The short tail of the Compact is very evident in this picture of a 1999 model.

113

The 323ti Compact presented a new and attractive development of the range . . .

*. . . and its appeal was undoubtedly
helped by these special alloy wheels.*

models which were the car's chosen rivals. BMW used them once again when a six-cylinder engine was at last introduced for the Compact models in 1997; the car was called the 323ti, and featured the six-cylinder M52 engine.

The last of the new body styles to appear was the Touring, which arrived in spring 1995 to take over from the outgoing E30 Touring models whose production had ceased the previous year. BMW claimed that the

Touring body had been planned from the start of the E36 project, and the longer roof and extra side windows certainly did not spoil the well-balanced styling of the saloon. At the rear, the big tailgate demanded slightly smaller tail light clusters than the saloon's, but the visual balance was not impaired by this change. From mid-1997, the BMW roundel on the tailgate was replaced by a larger type, as the original was considered insufficiently distinctive in some quarters!

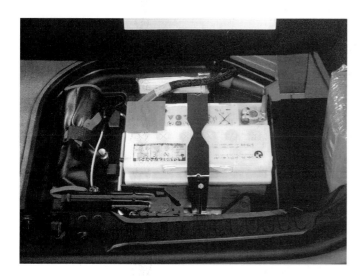

To improve weight distribution, the 323ti's battery was relocated at the rear of the car.

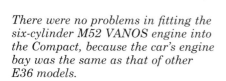
There were no problems in fitting the six-cylinder M52 VANOS engine into the Compact, because the car's engine bay was the same as that of other E36 models.

328i (1994–98)

Layout
Four-door saloon; coupé; Touring

Engine

Cylinders	Six
Bore × stroke	84mm × 84mm
Capacity	2793cc
Valves	Four per cylinder
Timing	Chain-driven twin ohc; VANOS variable valve timing
Compression ratio	10.2:1
Fuel injection	Bosch Motronic engine management system
Exhaust	Fitted with Lambda probe and three-way catalytic converter
Max. power	193bhp at 5300rpm
Max. torque	206lb/ft at 3950rpm

Transmission

Gearbox   Five-speed close-ratio manual

Ratios	Normal	five-speed overdrive automatic
First	4.20:1	3.67:1
Second	2.49:1	2.00:1
Third	1.66:1	1.41.1
Fourth	1.24:1	1.00:1
Fifth	1.00:1	0.74:1
Final drive	2.93:1	4.45:1

Suspension and Steering
As for 323i

Brakes
As for 323i

Dimensions
As for 323i, except unladen weight typically 1,395kg/3,075lb

Overall dimensions of the Touring were the same as the saloon's, but the load area was much more impressive than the rather cramped space of the old E30 Touring. Increased in width from 21.5in (550mm) to 35in (889mm), it promised an extra 12 per cent capacity increase, and was easily reached through the top-hinged tailgate. A one-third/two-thirds split folding rear seat and retractable luggage cover blind were part of the standard specification.

The Touring was eventually made available with six different drivetrains. They were those of the 318i, 318tds, 320i, 323i, 325tds and 328i. Like the Convertible, it remained in production after the E46 four-door saloons had replaced the mainstream E36 models in 1998.

THE 1996 FACELIFT

With the introduction of the replacement E46 models still two years away, the E36

Once again there was a Touring estate derivative, which this time offered rather more load space than its predecessor. Yet another design of ten-spoke alloy wheel is seen on this 320i model.

The Baur Topcabriolet

Early in 1994, BMW dealers in Germany began to offer a new version of the E36, created in conjunction with the Stuttgart coachbuilder Baur. Known as the BMW Baur TC or Topcabriolet, this was a cabrio-limousine conversion of the four-door saloon. Baur removed the roof and rear window, leaving the body sides intact and braced by a cross-bar between the central pillars. A three-position folding top was fitted. When stowed, this sat on the rear deck and did not intrude into the boot space.

It is not clear how many of these cars were built, but the conversion seems to have been fairly rare. In theory, the Topcabriolet was available as a conversion of a four-door E36 with any engine.

Baur offered this Top-cabriolet conversion from 1994.

318iS (1995–98)

As for earlier 318iS, except:

Layout
Two-door coupé; four-door saloon (1998 on)

Engine

Cylinders	Four
Bore × stroke	85mm × 83.5mm
Capacity	1895cc
Valves	Four per cylinder
Timing	Chain-driven ohc
Compression ratio	10.0:1
Fuel injection	Bosch DME 5.2 engine management system
Exhaust	Fitted with Lambda probe and three-way catalytic converter
Max. power	140bhp at 6000rpm
Max. torque	133lb/ft at 4300rpm

Transmission
Four-door saloon available only with manual gearbox

From September 1996, the E36 models had a mildly redesigned front end. Most obvious is the differently-shaped grille with its thicker, bright surrounds, as the upper picture shows. The newer car is on the left.

Alloy wheels eventually filtered down to the bottom of the range, as this 1997-model 316i Touring shows. The roof rails were an optional extra.

This 1997-model UK-market saloon has the revised front end styling and optional headlamp washers. Note also the attractive ten-spoke alloy wheels.

The Compact remained on sale after the new E46 models had replaced other E36 variants. Released in Britain in summer 1999 was this version, with a full-length fabric sunroof.

119

cars were given a minor facelift in September 1996 for the 1997 model-year. While there were also less visible changes – such as a new anti-theft system and pre-tensioners for the seat belts – the most noticeable aspect of the facelift was a revised front end. The nose of the car gained a more rounded grille with chunkier bright metal surrounds, and there was also a new panel around the headlamps. The main effect of this was to bring the cars more into line with the much more rounded noses of the E39 5 Series and E38 7 Series – and, of course, the E46 would also feature a more rounded nose when it arrived.

323i (1996 on) and 323ti Compact (1997 on)

Layout
Four-door saloon; coupé; convertible; Touring; Compact (323ti)

Engine

Cylinders	Six
Bore × stroke	84mm × 75mm
Capacity	2494cc
Valves	Four per cylinder
Timing	Chain-driven twin ohc; VANOS variable valve timing
Compression ratio	10.5.0:1
Fuel injection	Bosch Motronic engine management system
Exhaust	Fitted with Lambda probe and three-way catalytic converter
Max. power	170bhp at 5500rpm
Max. torque	181lb/ft at 3950rpm

Transmission
Five-speed close-ratio manual (ratios as for 316i) with 2.93:1 final drive, or five-speed overdrive automatic (ratios as for 320i)

Suspension and Steering
As for 316i

Brakes
As for 316i, but with ventilated front discs and 276mm solid discs at the rear

Dimensions
As for 320i, except unladen weight typically 1,385kg/3,053lb.

Natural Gas: the 316g

Since the late 1970s, BMW had been working on a zero-emissions vehicle, not least because legislation threatened for the end of the century in California demanded that a certain percentage of all road vehicles would fall into this category. One of the strands of the programme was the development of a car which would run on pure hydrogen (which can be produced from water by electrolysis through solar or electrical power), and a stage in the development of this was engines which would run on natural gas as well as on petrol.

In December 1995, BMW announced the availability in Germany of a natural gas-powered variant of the E36 range, called the 316g Compact. It was released alongside a 518g Touring version of the E34 range. Its engine was essentially the existing 318i type, but with changeover valves to allow it to run on compressed natural gas stored in an extra fuel tank. BMW claimed the changeover from petrol to gas and vice versa could be made seamlessly on the move, and that the car's fuel consumption on gas was the same as on petrol. The advantages were 20 per cent less carbon dioxide and 80 per cent fewer hydrocarbons in the exhaust gases.

The 316g Compact was never made available outside Germany because no other country had the necessary refuelling infrastructure. It was also substantially more expensive than the standard vehicle, and was not available for very long.

Production Totals

Four-cylinder E36
316i

	Saloon	Coupé	Compact
1989			
1990	4		
1991	48,986		
1992	63,152		
1993	63,877	6,854	120
1994	41,524	16,631	53,267
1995	37,735	10,911	50,905
1996	31,134	6,926	33,624
1997 } data not available
1998 }

318i

	Saloon	Convertible	Touring
1989	1		
1990	4,212		
1991	92,422		
1992	93,344		
1993	65,419	1	
1994	47,502	6,550	
1995	37,772	8,410	3,954
1996	22,738	7,244	11,391
1997 } data not available
1998 }

318iS

	Saloon	Coupé	Convertible	Compact
1993			13	
1994			4,294	10,384
1995	31	50	3,299	31,134
1996	5,447	13,003	3,583	22
1997 1998	} *data not available*			

318ti

	Compact
1995	60
1996	18,868
1997 1998	} *data not available*

Six-Cylinder E36

320i

	Saloon	Coupé	Convertible	Touring
1990	117			
1991	62,287	103		
1992	44,082	24,349		
1993	28,265	15,680		
1994	24,684	13,296	1,830	49
1995	20,998	8,378	6,875	10,215
1996	13,040	4,578	5,335	5,429
1997 1998	} *data not available*			

323i

	Saloon	Coupé	Convertible	Touring
1994	1	1		
1995	5,191	3,922	52	186
1996	9,042	5,301	38	1,909

325i

	Saloon	Coupé	Convertible
1989	2		
1990	3,999	3	
1991	50,914	2,611	
1992	32,358	31,351	20
1993	30,205	21,916	16,931
1994	26,058	19,106	15,184
1995	13,930	5,514	6,670
1996	*data not available*		

328i

	Saloon	Coupé	Convertible	Touring
1994	31	32	7	18

| 1995 | 13,577 | 12,873 | 9,401 | 4,302 |
| 1996 | 23,144 | 14,300 | 13,229 | 3,007 |

Four-Cylinder Diesel E36
318td Compact and 318tds Saloon and Touring

	Saloon	Touring	Compact
1994	6,669	1	39
1995	13,589	6,901	7,385
1996	10,615	7,669	7,445

Six-cylinder diesel E36
325td

	Saloon
1991	4,989
1992	19,679
1993	14,320
1994	9,096
1995	3,725
1996	1,828
1997 1998	} *data not available*

325tds

	Saloon	Touring
1993	9,175	
1994	18,509	1
1995	9,664	2,106
1996	6,485	4,055
1997 1998	} *data not available*	

CKD and SKD production

The E36 models were produced in both CKD (Completely Knocked Down) and SKD (Semi-Knocked Down) forms for overseas assembly. Assembly took place in Brazil, Indonesia, Malaysia, Mexico, the Philippines, South Africa, Thailand and Uruguay. The figures below are not included in the annual production figures given above.

1991	3,175
1992	15,856
1993	19,214
1994	21,536
1995	24,984
1996	22,308
1997 1998	} *data not available*

Annual Production Figures
These figures include CKD and SKD production.

	1989	1990	1991	1992	1993
Saloon	3	8,332	259,598	252,615	216,950
Coupé		3	2,754	94,353	85,959
Convertible				21	17,548

Compact					120
Total	3	8,335	262,352	346,989	320,577
	1994	1995	1996	1997	1998
Saloon	184,528	179,619	143,235	154,054	50,875
Coupé	83,701	69,402	51,133	42,669	29,861
Convertible	34,281	35,587	30,677	30,829	27,035
Compact	63,690	89,484	59,959	64,934	52,780
Touring	69	27,664	33,460	34,470	26,840
Total	366,269	401,756	318,464		

Note: Figures for 1997 and 1998 are for model-year and not for calendar year. They include CKD and SKD production, but exclude M3 models.

6   The E36 M3

The success of the E30 M3 ensured that an M3 version of the E36 range was inevitable right from the start, but BMW made their customers wait. The E30 M3 saloon ceased production in December 1990 and the last M3 cabriolet was built in July 1991. After that, there was a pause of more than a year until the new M3 made its bow at the October 1992 Paris Motor Show. There had been plenty of rumour and speculation about the new car in the meantime, of course, and BMW made no attempt to hide some of the prototype cars from journalists attending other company events over the summer of 1992.

There were two main reasons for the delay. The first was associated with the development of the car itself. BMW wanted to ensure that there were no remaining prob-

lems with the mainstream E36 range before the M3 entered production. This was a wise move: as the previous chapter explains, there were a number of quality-control problems in the early days of the E36, and it would have been disastrous to allow such problems to affect the M3 as well. The second reason for the delay in launching the M3 was that BMW wanted to make the maximum possible impact by launching the car with the sporty two-door coupé bodyshell first of all, and this shell was not scheduled to enter production until the end of 1991.

Just as the range of body types for the mainstream E36 models proliferated, so there was an increase in the number of body styles available for the E36 M3. The original two-door coupé was followed by the expected

The M3 designation, already a legend by the early 1990s, was applied first to a derivative of the E36 coupé. Note the special sills, spoiler, door mirror and wheels which helped to distinguish the car. In this publicity picture, taken on the old Brooklands banking, the pre-war 328 sports-racer in the background was intended to emphasize the M3's sporting heritage.

M3 (1992–95)

Layout
Coupé; convertible (1994 on); four-door saloon (1994 on)

Engine

Cylinders	Six
Bore × stroke	86 × 85.8mm
Capacity	2990cc
Valves	Four
Timing	Chain-driven twin ohc and VANOS variable valve timing
Compression ratio	10.8:1
Carburettor	Bosch Motronic M3.3 engine management system
Exhaust	Fitted with twin Lambda probes and three-way catalytic converter
Max. power	286bhp at 7000rpm (US models 240bhp)
Max. torque	231lb/ft at 3600rpm

Transmission

Gearbox	Five-speed close-ratio manual
Ratios	
First	4.20:1
Second	2.49:1
Third	1.66:1
Fourth	1.24:1
Fifth	1.00:1
Final drive	3.15:1 (US models 3.23:1)

Suspension and Steering

Suspension	As for 325i
Steering	Variable-ratio power-assisted
Wheels	7.5J × 17 or 8J × 17; 8.5J × 17 rear wheels optional on coupé, standard on convertible and saloon
Tyres	235/40 ZR 17

Brakes
As for 325i

Dimensions

Track	Front 1,4822mm/56in
	Rear 1,444mm/56.8in
Wheelbase	2,700mm/106.3in
Overall length	4,433mm/174.5in
Overall width	1,710mm/67.3in
Overall height	1,366mm/53.8in
Unladen weight	1,480kg/3,263lb

convertible version, and then rather unexpectedly by a four-door saloon edition. As late as 1996, there were even rumours that BMW was contemplating a further expansion of the range by introducing an M3 Compact with the current Evolution running-gear, but no such car ever appeared in the showrooms.

This expansion of the range did nothing but good for the M3. The E36 M3 was hot property from day one, and sales were so strong that the car quickly became the best-selling M car ever. There was no doubt that BMW had anticipated this, of course: the company was confident enough of high sales volumes to develop right-hand drive versions of the car this time, for sale in countries such as the UK. There were also special versions for the USA and – as with the original M3 – there were several limited editions.

THE ENGINE

Central to the original M3 had been its Motorsport-developed four-cylinder engine, and there was never any doubt that the character of the new M3 would also be defined by its power unit. However, BMW realized right from the beginning that a raw and highly-tuned four-cylinder would not be right for the new car, as its appeal was too limited. Market research had also made clear that a substantial part of the company's reputation as a car maker depended on its smooth and powerful six-cylinder engines. So the decision was taken that the new M3 should have a six-cylinder engine and that it should be an altogether more sophisticated piece of machinery than that fitted to the E30.

The Motorsport engine designers therefore started with the latest small-block six-cylinder M50 engine. The first move was to increase its swept volume by boring and stroking the block to give an eventual 2990cc. The twin overhead camshafts already operated four valves for each cylinder, so there was little to be done about the engine's breathing. Instead, work concentrated on the development of an ingenious variable valve timing system. This system,

called VANOS when it entered production, has already been described in Chapter 5, but it was developed first by the Motorsport division for the M3 engine.

Additional work provided the engine with a new dual-mass flywheel to improve the smoothness of its operation, and with twin catalytic converters, each one serving three cylinders. The Bosch DME M3.3 management system was programmed to suit the characteristics of the new engine, and the result was an absolute cracker of an engine, which pumped out 286bhp at 7000rpm and would run on to a 7,250rpm red line. Much more important, however, was the astonishingly flat torque curve which resulted from the use of the VANOS system. Conventional paper figures reveal that maximum torque of 236lb/ft was generated at 3600rpm, but what they do not show is that almost all of

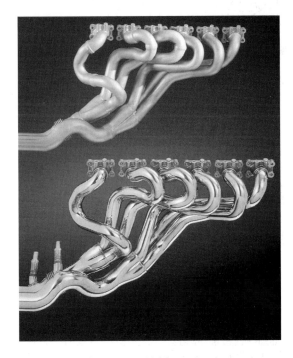

A tubular exhaust manifold was an important element in allowing the M3 engine to breathe effectively.

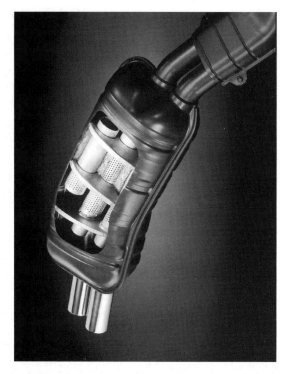

A free-flow silencer minimized the restrictive effect of the exhaust system on the M3.

this torque was available all the way from 3600rpm up to 5900rpm, giving blistering high-speed acceleration.

Yet discretion and refinement were to be the hallmarks of this second-generation M3. The top of the engine was not painted brightly in the Motorsport colours, as it had been on the earlier M3s. Instead, the cam covers had a purposeful-looking crackle-black finish, and the legend 'M Power' in raised letters said it all to anyone who took a look under the bonnet.

GEARBOX AND 'CHASSIS'

BMW knew that the E30 M3's racing-style gearchange gate with its dog-leg first would be a hindrance to increased sales: buyers wanted the extra performance associated with the M3 name, but without the penalty of unfamiliar driving controls. So for the E36 M3, a version of the latest close-ratio five-speed gearbox with direct top gear was chosen, allied to a 3.15:1 final drive and a 25 per cent limited-slip differential. While some buyers might well have been tempted by an automatic transmission, the view from BMW's marketing division was that the M3 image would be best served if the car was available only with a manual gearbox.

A great deal of work also went into the car's 'chassis' – its suspension, steering, brakes, wheels and tyres. Although the basic layout of the E36 suspension was not changed, several of the individual components were beefed up or changed in order to give the M3 a handling precision which would be in keeping with its performance. The front track arms were modified to give more caster in the steering, and the rear control arms were made thicker. Larger-diameter front and rear anti-roll bars were added, as were stronger stub-axles and spring plates, and enlarged rear wheel-bearings from the 8 Series coupés were fitted. The springs themselves were changed for progressive-rate types, and the dampers were stiffened by some 10 per cent over the ones used in the standard E36 coupé's M Technic suspension.

These changes were allied to 17in alloy wheels running on low-profile tyres. The standard rims were 7.5J types, but 8.5J versions were made optional for the rear wheels. Both sizes ran on 235/40 ZR 17 tyres. Needless to say, a special design of ten-spoke alloy wheel was developed as standard wear for the M3, but the car carried a space-saver spare rather than a full-size wheel and tyre.

These larger wheels allowed for the larger brakes so necessary to give adequate margins of safety in a high-performance car.

The discs themselves were over an inch larger in diameter than the standard E36 types, and were ventilated on both front and rear wheels. A larger master-cylinder was allied to a re-tuned ABS system to give the best possible braking. Meanwhile, the steering knuckles were reinforced to cope with the higher cornering forces that the car would generate when being driven enthusiastically and the Motorsport engineers chose a speed-sensitive power-assisted system which decreased the degree of assistance available at higher speeds, in order to give the driver more feel.

STYLING, INTERIOR AND OPTIONS

The revised suspension made the M3 coupé sit 30mm (1.2in) closer to the ground than the standard two-door E36, and the big alloy wheels on their 40-section tyres added to the sporting appearance of the car. However, this was no extrovert machine in the E30 M3 mould; this was a discreet machine in the mould of the 'Q-car' M5 businessman's express. Some commentators argued that it was actually too discreet – but the high acceptance and high sales proved that BMW had got the balance fundamentally right.

Starting at the front, the M3 was dressed up with a deep front spoiler with a pronounced lip extension. The spoiler contained a mesh grille painted in the body colour and a pair of long-range driving lamps. The body sills had been re-shaped with a 'crossover' sculpted pattern, which may have made some difference to the aerodynamics but was primarily an aid to distinguishing the car from lesser E36 coupés. The doors carried attractively-shaped rear view mirrors, each of which stood out from the body on a pair of narrow, aerodynamically profiled

legs. The rear valance was deeper than the standard E36 type, and featured extensions designed to improve the airflow. Finally, there was a discreet M3 badge on the boot lid – but nothing on the grille, where the earlier M3 had proudly displayed the same badge.

The interior was as heavily based on the standard article as was the body. However, there were M logos on the instrument binnacle and the gear knob, and the instruments had red markings. Instead of the fuel economy gauge fitted to other E36s, the M3 carried an oil temperature gauge. An external temperature gauge was also standard, and twin airbags were standard for all markets. The standard steering wheel could be replaced at extra cost by a leather-rimmed Motorsport type which, of course, contained the driver's airbag.

Special front seats were part of the package. Very obviously sports-oriented in design, they had an adjustable upper third and their headrests were also adjustable for height. Their cushions could be extended to improve thigh support as well. Upholstery was cloth on the wearing surfaces with a suede-like material for the wraparound sides of the front seats and the edges of the rear bench. An on-board computer, central locking and electric windows were all part of the standard package.

Leather upholstery, electrically-adjustable front seats, air conditioning, and a cruise control were all on the options list. Metallic paint, an anti-theft alarm system and the wider rear wheels already mentioned were the other extra-cost items available when customers ordered a new M3 coupé.

THE M3 CONVERTIBLE

A convertible version of the M3 was only to be expected after the success of the earlier

How Fast was the E36 M3?

The E36 M3 was a bigger and heavier car than its E30 predecessor, and the fact that it was so much faster – even with the standard catalytic converter – speaks volumes for its remarkable engine. The figures below bear comparison with those for the E30 M3, on page 87.

	0–60mph	Standing $\frac{1}{4}$-mile	Max speed	Source
M3 coupé	5.4 sec	13.9 sec	162mph* (261km/h)	*Autocar*
M3 convertible	5.7 sec	14.4 sec	155mph (250km/h)	*Autocar*
M3 saloon	5.5 sec	14.3 sec	156mph (251km/h)	*Autocar*
M3 Evolution	5.4 sec	N/A	155mph (250km/h)	*BMW*

* This figure was achieved in spite of a limiter in the engine management system which should not have allowed the car to exceed 155mph!

As on the E30s, a convertible M3 was also made available. It was an extraordinarily attractive car, if not quite as fast as the M3 coupé.

M3 cabriolet, and it arrived in spring 1994, several months after the convertible E36 body had been announced.

The car brought few surprises. It combined the new soft-top body with the drivetrain and suspension of the M3 coupé in a svelte package which weighed some 80kg (176lb) more than the fixed-roof car and was rather less aerodynamic. As a result, it was a little slower off the mark – but an M3 convertible was still fast enough to need a speed limiter in its engine management system which kept the maximum down to 155mph (250km/h).

Some of that extra weight came from the M3 convertible's power-operated soft top, a feature which was not even optional on lesser E36 convertibles. The presence of this made quite clear that BMW's marketing objectives with this car were less associated with the promise of high performance than with the promise of a high specification. The interior reflected this, with nappa leather as the standard upholstery, and the forged and polished 17in alloy wheels again made clear that BMW believed appearance would be an important factor in the car's appeal.

The M3 convertible came with the wider 8.5J rear wheels, which were only optional on the M3 coupé, as standard. It also had a slightly different front spoiler, without the prominent lip. For those who wanted to use it as a closed car during inclement weather, a hugely expensive removable hard top was also available.

THE M3 SALOON

Some people were surprised to see a four-door saloon variant of the M3 announced in summer 1994, but there was a certain ruthless logic to its introduction. On the one hand, BMW were constantly looking at ways of broadening the appeal and increasing the sales of the M3 – all without diminishing its exclusivity, of course. On the other hand, the M5 had shown only too clearly that there was a market for a high-performance car which retained all the practicality of a family saloon. The M3 saloon, priced well below the M5, brought the availability of such a car down to a new clientele.

Once again, the specification of the car gave a clear indication of BMW's thinking. Above all, this was to be a practical everyday car, and so its standard leather seats came with electric heating elements for the driver and front passenger, and the front door trims contained storage pockets. The suspension, too, had been retuned for greater comfort.

Equally important was that it should be discreet, although those who knew what to look for should be able to recognize it for what it was immediately. So although the side skirts of the M3 saloon were less eye-catching than those of the other M3 models, the car still had the deep front spoiler with its central grille. This spoiler was the same as that on the convertible, without the prominent lip advertising the car's performance pretensions. As for the wheels, these were unique five-spoke alloys. To the casual observer, they were simply attractive cosmetic items, but to the more knowledgeable, they made clear straight away that this was not a car to be trifled with. For, despite a weight increase of around 15kg (33lb), the M3 saloon was as fast as its coupé equivalent.

Finally, the interior had a few cosmetic touches designed to add to the car's exclusivity. The standard leather upholstery has already been mentioned; in addition, there was wood trim on the instrument panel and steering wheel, and the door release handles were chromed.

M3 saloon, coupé and convertible are seen here lined up in Germany.

The Right-Hand Drive M3

The first M3s with right-hand drive were built in August 1993, nearly a year after the car had been announced in left-hand drive form at the Paris Motor Show.

Sales in the UK, which was the right-hand-drive M3's largest market, were as follows:

1993	270
1994	999
1995	1,409
1996	
1997	
1998	

THE M3 IN THE USA

The USA was potentially one of the best markets for the new M3 and the car was announced there – initially in coupé form only – in January 1994. Convertible and four-door saloon versions followed later, as in Europe.

Unfortunately, the full-house M3 engine was not compatible with federal emissions regulations, and so a less powerful version of the 2990cc six-cylinder was used. The major differences lay in the cylinder head; power was reduced to 240bhp, but an even broader spread of torque and lower gearing ensured that the car's standing-start acceleration was very similar to that of European models.

THE M3 GT

In November 1994, BMW introduced a new limited-production version of the M3 coupé known as the M3 GT built, essentially, to comply with 1995 Le Mans regulations. It featured stiffened and lowered suspension, a 295bhp version of the 3ltr engine, a front air dam with a splitter, and a rear spoiler.

All 396 M3 GT models were made with left-hand drive, and all were painted in dark green. They came with leather upholstery as standard, and some interior trim parts were made of Kevlar.

THE M3 LIGHTWEIGHT

Even though the 240bhp US-specification M3 was fast enough for all reasonable road requirements, it was not fast enough for those who wanted to use it on the race tracks. BMW's importers argued the case for a limited-production model intended for competition use, and the factory obliged with a car known as the M3 Lightweight. The first Lightweights were built towards the end of January 1995.

Broadly speaking, the M3 Lightweight was a stripped-out version of the regular M3 coupé, but in addition to losing such items as the sunroof, air conditioning, radio and sound insulation, it carried aluminium doors. The result was a car which was some 91kg (200lb) lighter than the standard article, despite the extra weight of a strut brace above the engine and a cross-brace below it.

The Lightweight also looked special, being available only in Alpine White with the Motorsport colours in a chequered flag pattern diagonally across opposite front and rear quarters. For good measure, there was a BMW Motorsport International logo on the door sills, on the side protection strip and on a glovebox-mounted plaque. Forged alloy double-spoke wheels were fitted, and there was a GT-style rear spoiler. The front spoiler was a GT-style item with a unique spring-loaded extendable splitter which could be removed for street use. Inside, the Lightweight had special seats and trim, with carbon fibre panelling on the console, door sills and facia.

The M3 Lightweight had the standard 240bhp US-specification engine, although legend has it that the cars were equipped with the best of the engines which came off the assembly lines, in order to guarantee maximum performance. The rest of the drivetrain, with its 3.23:1 axle gearing, was to standard US specification. Estimated figures suggest that the cars were capable of reaching 60mph from rest in 5.8 seconds.

Just eighty-five examples of the M3 Lightweight were built for the US market, although BMW records show that a total of 116 cars were made in all. What happened to the other thirty-one cars is not clear.

THE AUSTRALIAN M3-R

The M3-R was put together by BMW Australia purely for competitors in the country's popular GT Production racing series. It was developed in collaboration with Frank Gardner, whose BMW M Team campaigned racing versions in the Australian Production GT series. There were just fifteen cars in all, of which four were built up as works racers while the other eleven were sold to well-heeled enthusiasts who could lay claim to an Australian motor racing licence. The R in the car's name stood for Racing.

The cars started life as standard M3 coupés, built at BMW's Dingolfing plant in Germany. Out in Australia, they were stripped of all 'unnecessary equipment', as the specification sheet had it: that meant the sound deadening, the spare wheel, the tools, the boot trim and rear trim, the back seat and even the M3 badges. The weight saving was around 200kg (441lb).

The suspension was replaced by Motorsport Group N parts, and the brakes by special AP four-pot racing calipers front and rear. The standard wheels were replaced by 17in BBS cross-spoke alloys, with a 7.5J size at the front and an 8.5J size at the rear. These were equipped with Michelin Pilot SX tyres, size 235/45Z R 17 all round.

Next came a European-style M3 GT adjustable front splitter, and a Class II Evolution two-part racing rear wing with flaps. The standard M3 gearbox was replaced by a slicker-shifting five-speed type and – most important of all – the engine was breathed on to give an additional 39bhp over standard. The resulting 326bhp at 6000rpm was achieved by means of new camshafts, shorter inlet trumpets and a lightened flywheel, plus, of course, a remapped chip. Without the restrictor used to safeguard the engines, power was claimed to be as high as 395bhp. An AP Racing twin sintered plate racing clutch with a heavy-duty release bearing, a twin-rotor oil pump and a surge-resisting sump were also fitted.

Both restricted and unrestricted versions of the car were good for approximately 180mph (290km/h) all-out. BMW Australia claimed that the restricted M3-R could reach 62mph (100km/h) from rest in just 5.4sec, while the unrestricted car needed just 5sec.

THE M3 EVOLUTION

In October 1995, BMW introduced a revised version of the E36 M3 under the name of the M3 Evolution. Initially available only in two-door coupé form, it was followed by convertible and saloon forms early in 1996. Right-hand drive production began more

The M3 Evolution coupé gained these stunning new alloy wheels.

or less simultaneously, and UK sales of all three M3 Evolution models began in February 1996.

The most important changes that the Evolution models brought lay in the drivetrain and 'chassis', as described below, but the coupé and convertible models also had the aluminium doors seen on earlier competitions variants of the M3. Outward recognition features were the clear indicator lenses, a third stop lamp behind the rear window glass and a matt black grille in the front air dam. There were new wheels, too, each model getting its own unique type but all of them wearing 225/45 R 17 tyres on the front and 245/40 R 17s on the rear.

The M3 Evolution Coupé had M Sports seats with integrated head restraints, and rode on the M-tuned sports suspension. It boasted ten-spoke 'M-Style Double Spoke II' alloy wheels, and had a space-saver spare as before. The same suspension was used on the M3 Evolution Convertible, this time with 'M-Style Double Spoke' five-spoke alloy wheels. The convertible also came with leather upholstery as standard, a rear seat armrest, and metallic paint. As for the saloon, the ordinary sports suspension was standard, with 'M-Contour II' five-spoke alloy wheels. Saloons also had leather upholstery as standard, with a rear seat armrest and a front centre armrest. There was burr walnut trim on the centre console, on the gearknob and door pulls, and electric windows were once again standard.

A bigger engine was the real heart of the M3 Evolution. This had been developed over a period of three years by the team who had also developed the BMW V12 for the McLaren F1 supercar. Both bore and stroke had been increased to give a swept volume of 3201cc although, remarkably for a BMW engine, the stroke was now greater than the bore, giving an undersquare configuration. The engine now boasted Double-VANOS, with variable valve timing on the exhaust as well as the inlet camshaft. Bigger inlet valves, lightweight pistons and a reworked exhaust manifold were further changes, and the conrods were now graphite-coated to reduce friction. The engine also incorporated an improved dual-mass flywheel, a modified vibration damper and a second oil pump to guarantee full lubrication when the car was cornering hard.

BMW made much of the new engine management system that made its first appearance here, too. Known as the MSS 50 type, this had been developed by BMW with help from Siemens and was capable of monitoring and adjusting a huge variety of engine functions. Its success was perhaps best measured by the reduced fuel consumption of the new engine, which was nevertheless considerably more powerful than its predecessor. Maximum power was quoted as 321bhp at 7400rpm, and maximum torque as 258 lb/ft at 3250rpm – although, as on the earlier M3 engine, the torque delivery was far more even and far more widely spread than that peak figure suggests. Top speed of the M3 Evolution models was still restricted to 155mph (249kph), but the 0–62mph (100km/h) standing-start time came down to around 5.5sec, and BMW engineers estimated that 180mph (290km/h) would have been possible without the speed limiter.

The M3 Evolution models also had a new

This right-hand drive M3 Evolution Coupé shows some interesting differences from the saloon equivalent. Note the different seat stitching and the absence of wood trim. The handle on the side of the driver's seat releases a catch so that the backrest can be tipped forwards, allowing rear seat passengers to get in or out of this two-door car.

M3 Evolution (1995–98)

As for earlier M3, except:

Engine

Cylinders	Six
Bore × stroke	86.4 × 91mm (US models 86.4 × 89.6mm)
Capacity	3201cc (US models 3152cc)
Valves	Four
Timing	Chain-driven twin ohc and double-VANOS variable valve timing
Compression ratio	11.3:1 (US models 10.5:1)
Engine management	BMW MSS 50 system
Exhaust	Fitted with twin Lambda probes and three-way catalytic converter
Max. power	321bhp at 7400rpm (US models 243bhp)
Max. torque	258lb/ft at 3250rpm (US models 236lb/ft at 3800rpm)

Transmission

Gearbox	Six-speed overdrive manual (US models retain five-speed from earlier M3)
Ratios	
First	4.23:1
Second	2.51:1
Third	1.67:1
Fourth	1.23:1
Fifth	1.00:1
Sixth	0.83:1
Final drive	3.23:1

Wheels and Tyres

225/45 R 17 front tyres on 7.5J × 17 wheels and 245/50 R 17 rear tyres on 8.5J × 17 wheels

The subtle use of wood trim gave the M3 Evolution a suitably up-market feel. On this right-hand drive car, there is wood around the gear lever gaiter, on the gear knob, on the handbrake grip and on the door-pull.

New multi-spoke alloy wheels were the quickest way of distingushing an M3 Evolution from its smaller-engined forebears.

gearbox, this time a six-speed manual type derived from the M5 gearbox. The great advantage of this was that it offered five closely-spaced ratios for optimum acceleration, plus an overdrive top gear to minimize fuel consumption at cruising speeds. However, other issues had also had an influence on BMW's decision to switch from the earlier five-speed gearbox. Among these were the introduction of drive-by noise regulations in some markets and the knowledge that other manufacturers were already preparing to introduce six-speed gearboxes. As a marketing tool, the six-speed gearbox also had considerable potential!

As before, a 25 per cent limited-slip differential was standard, and in this case the component was the same as that used in the M5. Braking had been uprated by the use of the M5's racing-type floating brake calipers in tandem with a new ABS system. This, the Teves Mk IV type, had been developed espe-

cially for the M3 Evolution. Handling and steering had also received attention for the revised cars. There were new springs and dampers, while increased caster of the front wheels improved straight-line stability and reduced oversteer. The steering itself was also quicker than before, but no longer had the speed-sensitive weighting.

THE US M3 EVOLUTION

Once again, the USA got a slightly different version of the new car. Instead of the new 3201cc engine, the US M3 Evolution was equipped with a special short-stroke version of 3152cc – although the engine was still undersquare. This retained the 10.5:1 compression ratio of the earlier M3 engine, and delivered 243bhp at 6000rpm, with a maximum torque of 236lb/ft at 3800rpm. In comparison to the European figures of

Heart of the matter: the 3.2ltr M3 Evolution engine was beautifully packaged, as always.

The 3.2ltr engine in the M3 Evolution models offered dramatic improvements over the 3ltr type which it replaced, as these graphs show. On the left is the torque graph, and on the right the power graph. In each case, the Evolution engine is represented by the upper line.

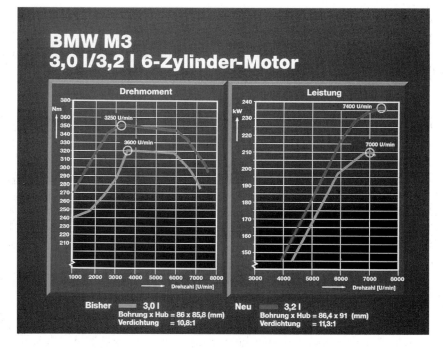

321bhp at 7400rpm and 258lb/ft at 3250rpm, this was quite a tame animal, although it still offered worthy performance. US M3 Evolution models also retained the five-speed gearbox with its direct-drive top gear, and did not get the new six-speed type.

SUBSEQUENT DEVELOPMENTS

In September 1996, the M3 models benefitted from the minor modifications introduced right across the E36 range at that time. They also gained a new M Sport airbag steering

With the M3 Evolution came a six-speed overdrive gearbox, which still offered the close ratios of the earlier five-speed type. Note the M logo on the gear knob.

An M3 Compact

The Compact version of the E36 was never turned into a production M3, but BMW Motorsport did build one solitary M3 Compact during 1996. Officially, the car was a present to the German magazine *Auto, Motor und Sport*, to celebrate its fiftieth year in print. Unofficially, it was a way of guaging public reaction to the idea of an M3 Compact.

The car had a standard M3 engine and five-speed gearbox, allied to the rear axle from the Z3M. In a package 9in (230mm) shorter and 150kg (331lb) lighter than the M3 saloon, it delivered 0–60mph in 5.2 seconds. Top speed of the M3 Compact was limited, as usual, to 155mph (250km/h).

wheel and became available with the new Sequential M Gearbox.

The Sequential M Gearbox – SMG for short – had actually been announced a couple of months earlier, in July; in practice, however, it did not become available in Europe until March 1997, and it was March 1998 before examples reached the UK. Essentially, the SMG was a control system which provided a clutchless racing-style sequential gearshift for the six-speed manual gearbox. This brought the convenience of an automatic transmission to the car, because the computer-controlled system gave fully automatic gearchanges when the

The Sequential M Gearbox announced in 1996 had this neat gearshift. The indicator on the left of the panel ahead of it shows the gate pattern . . .

There was also a gearshift indicator on the instrument panel, at the bottom of the rev counter.

lever was in the Economy mode. In Sports mode, however, changes were made manually – if the lever was pushed forwards the gearbox changed up, and if it was pulled backwards, the box changed down. Thus, driving enthusiasts were not denied the pleasure of a manual gearchange.

The final change of note to the E36 M3 models came in September 1997. For the 1998 model-year, steel door skins replaced the lightweight alloy panels which had been used since the start of M3 Evolution production. By this time, the end of production was in sight. M3 saloon production was the first to go, as the 50,000th M3 came off the line at BMW's Regensburg assembly plant on 12 December 1997. This last M3 saloon was delivered to the Bavarian police as an

In late 1997, the final E36 M3 saloon was delivered to the Police in BMW's home state of Bavaria for use as a patrol car. The car was also the 50,000th M3 to be built. All E36 M3s had clear front indicator lenses, and these became a popular accessory among those who wanted an M3 but could not quite afford one . . .

There was of course an M3 Evolution version of the convertible as well . . .

. . . and customer demand led also to an M3 four-door saloon.

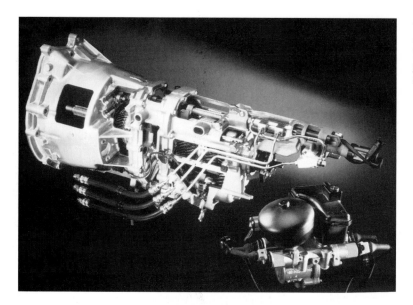

The six-speed Sequential M Gearbox itself looked like this. The components in the foreground were located in the engine bay . . .

. . . as is clear from this ghosted diagram.

The M3 Evolution GT

In 1998, BMW marked the end of M3 production with a limited edition of just fifty M3 Evolution GT cars. Painted in Imola Red, these cars had special interior trim and additional features such as front and rear M Class II GT spoilers, side and passenger airbags, an electric sunroof, electric seats and a Harmon Kardon stereo system.

Autobahn patrol car, and its special features included an increased luggage capacity, a power take-off, dual rear view mirrors, a roof mounted signal and communication system, firearm supports in the roof lining, and a Police radio. Production of the other E36 M3 variants wound down slowly after that, in preparation for the introduction of a new E46 M3 model.

M3 Production

The figures given below are for calendar-year. Note that during 1995, production was of M3 Evolution models from late summer; 1995 figures therefore are the totals for both types of car built that year.

	Coupé	Convertible	Saloon	KD models*	Total
1992	470			50	520
1993	6,080	3		632	6,715
1994	9,289	1,118	288	66	10,761
1995	9,828	860	1,282	0	11,970
1996	6,896	1,248	3,639	168	11,951

The total figures for 1997 and 1998 were 11,933 and 6,118, respectively; individual model breakdowns were not available as this book went to press. As these figures are for model-year, the 1996 figures necessarily duplicate a proportion of those given above for the 1996 calendar year.

*KD assembly of M3 models was in South Africa, and began in November 1992. From then until 1994, assembly was from SKD kits; from 1996, assembly was from CKD.

7 Fourth Generation
– the E46 Models

The E36 range was BMW's biggest seller in the early 1990s, and for that reason its replacement was destined to be critical to the company's performance. Announced at the Geneva Motor Show in March 1997, the fourth-generation 3 Series – coded E46 internally – had started life on the computer screens of BMW's design engineers some three and a half years earlier. The project was overseen by Dr Wolfgang Ziebart and, as was to be expected, CKD assembly was designed in from the start. The press reactions to the first cars showed that BMW had amply fulfilled its design aim of improving vehicle dynamics, safety, cost of ownership, technology and quality.

Once again, a four-door saloon model was chosen as the core of the range, and BMW planned to introduce the smaller-selling variants progressively at approximately twelve-monthly intervals after the saloon's launch. So the coupé – biggest seller of the niche-market E36 models – arrived in 1999, leaving Convertible, Compact and Touring types to follow. An M3 was also planned, although buyers were to be made to wait for

The E46 design brought elements of the larger 5 Series styling down to the entry-level range, but remained distinctive. This is a 318i model, with the relatively plain seven-spoke alloy wheels used on the cheaper cars.

More expensive E46 models came with these five-spoke alloy wheels. In this picture, note how the bonnet wraps over the front of the car to incorporate the grille – a borrowing from the E39 5 Series. The scalloped panel below the headlamps was a subtle but readily recognizable distinguishing feature.

All the first E46 models were four-door saloons, although even the cheapest models looked far less stodgy than entry-level E36 cars had done at the beginning of the decade.

it in the fashion by now almost traditional to BMW. Not only did this give the company time to develop the car at its own pace after any problems with the early bread-and-butter models had been detected, but it also created a very healthy pent-up demand for the car before it was released.

BMW publicity insisted that every nut and bolt on the E46 was new, except for the sump plug. While this was not strictly true – some engines, for example, were developments of earlier designs – it did help to make the point that the car was not just a facelift of the E36. While it most certainly had a strong family resemblance, the E46 was actually a rather bigger car than its predecessor. This was perhaps partly a response to the increase in size of its direct rival from Mercedes-Benz, the W202 C-class that had

replaced the W201 190 range in 1994. Arguably, however, the increase in size was just as much to do with the desperate need to increase rear legroom in the 3 Series. Though it was undoubtedly bigger than the outgoing E36, the E46 did not really look bigger, and its new size did not disrupt the BMW model hierarchy because the E46 remained 30cm (nearly 12in) shorter than the E39 5 Series saloons.

In practice, the size increase amounted to 38mm (1.5in) in the length, of which 25mm (0.98in) went into the wheelbase. This was supplemented by a width increase of 41mm (1.6in) and a height increase of 22mm (0.86in). These revised dimensions allowed for wider tracks to improve the car's feeling of solidity on the move, and made their own contribution to the creation of a bodyshell

---

316i (1999 on)

Layout
Four-door saloon; others TBA

Engine

Cylinders	Four
Bore × stroke	83.5 × 85mm
Capacity	1895cc
Timing	Chain-driven ohc
Compression ratio	9.7:1
Engine management	BMS 46 system
Exhaust	Fitted with catalytic converter
Max. power	105bhp at 5300rpm
Max. torque	122lb/ft at 2500rpm

Transmission

Gearbox	Five-speed close-ratio manual	
Ratios	Normal	Four-speed overdrive automatic
First	4.23:1	2.40:1
Second	2.52:1	1.47:1
Third	1.66:1	1.00:1
Fourth	1.22:1	0.72:1
Fifth	1.00:1	
Final drive	3.23:1	4.44:1

Suspension and Steering

Front	Independent with MacPherson struts, coil springs and anti-roll bar
Rear	Multi-link with coil springs and anti-roll bar
Steering	Power-assisted rack and pinion, with 15.5:1 ratio
Wheels	6.5J × 15
Tyres	195/65 R 15

Brakes

Type	Servo-assisted with dual hydraulic circuit and ABS with CBC
Size	Front 286mm ventilated discs
Rear	280mm solid discs

Dimensions

Track	Front 1,481mm (58.31in)
	Rear 1,488mm (58.58in)
Wheelbase	2730mm (107.5in)
Overall length	4471mm (176in)
Overall width	1739mm (68.5in)
Overall height	1415mm (55.7in)
Unladen weight	1,360–1,395kg (2,998–3,075lb), depending on specification

---

which was 70 per cent stiffer in torsion than that of the outgoing model. Perhaps even more critically, however, they allowed the front wheels to be pushed even further forwards than on the E36, and for the engine to be moved further back in order

318i (1997 on) and 318Ci (1999 on)

As for 316i, except:

Layout
Four-door saloon; two-door coupé; others TBA

Engine
Max. power   118bhp at 5500rpm
Max. torque   133lb/ft at 3900rpm

Final Drive
3.38:1 final drive with manual gearbox

Wheels and Tyres
Saloon as for 316i; coupé has 7J × 16 wheels, with 205/55 R 16 tyres.

Dimensions
Saloon as for 316i
Coupé as for 316i, except:
Overall length   4,488mm (176.69in)
Overall width   1,757mm (69.2in)
Overall height   1,369mm (53.9in)

Despite the relatively compact overall dimensions of the E46 the boot was deep and capacious.

to achieve a near-perfect 50/50 weight distribution. This in turn, of course, had a beneficial impact on the handling of the car.

As already noted, the overall styling of the car made it instantly recognizable as a BMW, and as the smallest model in the range. While certain features had filtered down from the E39 5 Series, such as the integration of the kidney grille into the bonnet, the car still retained its own identity. It was still recognizably a BMW, too, even without that famous grille: early prototypes had been partially disguised with blacked-out grilles borrowed from the products of BMW's Rover subsidiary, but that had not fooled the spy photographers! The familiar kick in the trailing edge of the rear window was still there, the L-shaped rear lamp clusters were familiar BMW practice, and even the

Stepped tail light units were an idea borrowed from earlier large BMWs, while a spoiler was neatly integrated into the trailing edge of the boot lid.

glassed-over headlamps were distinguished for the casual observer only by means of a shaped panel at their lower edge.

Safety had been a very important consideration in the design of the E46, and to that end its bodyshell made extensive use of high-strength steel. The front and rear deformation zones had also been carefully designed, and the end result was a body claimed to be 60 per cent stiffer and more stable than its E36 equivalent. BMW publicity also claimed that the E46 bodyshell could absorb two and a half times as much collision energy as its E30 ancestor of ten years earlier. Side impact protection was provided by strong, interlocking diagonal bars in all four doors.

320d (1997 on)	
As for 318i, except:	
Engine	
Cylinders	Four
Bore × stroke	88 × 84mm
Capacity	1951cc
Timing	Chain-driven twin ohc
Compression ratio	19:1
Fuel injection	Common-rail high-pressure
Max. power	136bhp at 4000rpm
Max. torque	206lb/ft at 1750rpm
Transmission	
Gearbox	Five-speed close-ratio manual
Ratios	
First	5.09:1
Second	2.80:1
Third	1.76:1
Fourth	1.25:1
fifth	1.00:1
Final drive	2.47:1
Brakes	
276mm ventilated discs at the rear	

In addition to bodyshell strength, the E46 protected its occupants with a whole collection of safety belt and airbag systems. All four main belts were fitted with latch tensioners and free limiters, and those on the front seats were height-adjustable for the best possible fit and consequently the best possible occupant retention. Every model in the range also came with no fewer than six airbags as standard. The usual front airbags for driver and front seat passenger were supplemented by a side airbag in each front door and by an ITS head-height side airbag. Side airbags for the rear doors could be ordered at extra cost.

A sensor in the front passenger seat ensured that the airbags on that side of the car would not be activated if the seat was not occupied, and BMW promised for later a sophisticated system to detect whether a child seat was in use at the front. This followed a number of reported cases where the deployment of passenger's side airbags had injured or killed children in child seats strapped to the front passenger seat of a car.

The interior of the new car offered around 1.5in (38mm) of extra legroom for the rear seat passengers, which was certainly a step in the right direction. The seats themselves, front and rear, were newly designed and their upholstery made a contribution to the airy and spacious feel of the passenger cabin. The instrument panel was instantly recognizable as a BMW design, but it was set in a new dashboard which flowed round to marry up with the front door trims. New 'waterfall' instrument illumination cunningly created a 3D illusion of greater space within the car at night, and traditional instrument lighting bulbs were replaced by LEDs that were expected to last the life of the car. The new dashboard came with an integrated radio-cassette unit (to deter thieves) with CD preparation. The

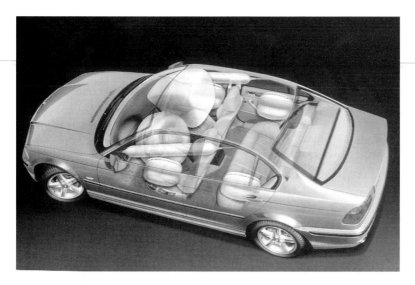

Safety had also been central to the E46 design brief, and this illustration shows the various airbags which were available on the car's introduction – although, for the most part, at extra cost.

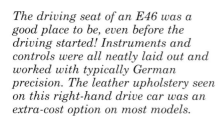

The driving seat of an E46 was a good place to be, even before the driving started! Instruments and controls were all neatly laid out and worked with typically German precision. The leather upholstery seen on this right-hand drive car was an extra-cost option on most models.

familiar BMW Check Control functions-check system was present, and all cars came with the convenience of Car Memory and Key Memory. Car Memory allowed the central lighting, optional air conditioning, and central locking to be programmed in advance, while Key Memory was activated by the ignition key and adjusted a whole range of items to suit the owner of that key. Up to four sets of settings could be pre-programmed for each car, each one using a different key.

The less visible areas of the E46 had also been substantially redesigned compared to their predecessors on the E36 range. As already noted, the stiffer bodyshell allowed the suspension to work better, the rearward mounting of the engine gave near-perfect front-to-rear weight distribution, and the longer wheelbase and wider track contributed to better poise and balance. Following on from the example of the E39 5 Series, aluminium suspension parts were used to reduce unsprung weight to the benefit of ride

One of the big failings of earlier 3 Series cars had been a lack of room for rear seat passengers. With the E46, BMW addressed this problem.

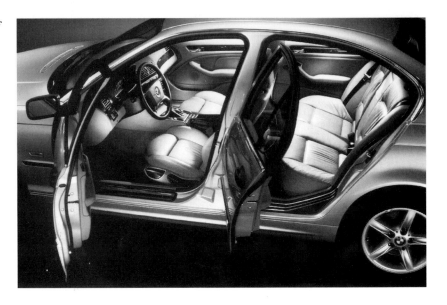

320i (1997 on) and 320Ci (1999 on)	
As for 318i, except:	
Engine	
Cylinders	Six
Bore × Stroke	66mm bore × 80mm
Capacity	1991cc
Valves	Four per cylinder
Timing	Chain-driven twin ohc and Double-VANOS variable valve timing
Compression ratio	11.0:1
Engine management system	BMW DMS 46
Exhaust	Fitted with twin catalytic converters
Max. power	150bhp at 5900rpm
Max. torque	140lb/ft at 3500rpm
Brakes	
276mm ventilated discs at the rear	

323i (1997 on) and 323Ci (1999 on)	
As for 318i, except:	
Engine	
Cylinders	Six
Bore × stroke	75 × 84mm
Capacity	2494cc
Valves	Four per cylinder
Timing	Chain-driven twin ohc and Double-VANOS variable valve timing
Compression ratio	10.5:1
Engine management system	BMW DMS 46
Exhaust	Fitted with twin catalytic converters
Max. power	170bhp at 5500rpm
Max torque	181lb/ft at 3500rpm
Brakes	
276mm ventilated discs at the rear	

quality, although the basic design of the suspension was not radically different. ABS brakes were standard, as was power-assisted rack-and-pinion steering, and both braking and traction control aids were available – though some only optionally or on top models.

Options, of course, came in all shapes and sizes. The standard alloy wheels had seven

The E46: How Safe?

BMW put a great deal of work into 'passive safety' during the development of the E46, and these efforts were vindicated in some independent tests carried out by the German magazine *auto, motor & sport* during 1999.

An E46 was subjected to a frontal crash replicating the Euro-NCAP (European New Car Assessment Program), with an impact at 64km/h (40mph) into a 40 per cent offset, deformable barrier with a driver and front passenger on board. In this impact, both driver and passenger were virtually uninjured. The vital head and neck areas were so well protected by the airbags and belt systems that the magazine concluded: 'Never before has *auto, motor & sport* measured such low strain to the neck' . . . and this regardless of vehicle class.

A side impact test was conducted at 32km/h (20mph) against an iron pole. In this impact, the ITS head airbag was found to have a dramatic effect. It reduced the HIC (Head Injury Criterion) score to just 389, compared to a score of more than 2500 without ITS. Without ITS, this impact would almost certainly not have been survivable.

In overall conclusion, the magazine noted that, 'Occupant protection in the new 3 Series is at such a high standard that only marginal improvements are conceivable.'

Handling was of course first-class, as was by now traditional for the 3 Series.

spokes on the petrol cars and five on the 320d, but they could be replaced by stylish multi-spoke alloy wheels which took their design cue from Alpina. These were designed to run on lower-profile tyres. Other options included AIC rain-sensing wipers, Park Distance Control, Xenon headlights, inte-grated child seats, automatic air conditioning, a windscreen which reflected infra-red rays to reduce interior temperatures, a multi-function steering wheel, automatic air recirculation to cut out pollutants, a dashboard monitor for satellite navigation, computer and hi-fi systems, and a lower-level

This ghosted drawing of an E46 saloon shows the essential elements of power train and suspension.

Among the desirable options was the BMW Navigation System, seen here neatly integrated into the centre console of a right-hand drive E46.

navigation system. Some of these were destined to become standard on the more expensive models, or to become part of special equipment packages.

THE ENGINES

At the launch of the E46 models, BMW introduced only five engine variants. These consisted of a single four-cylinder in the 318i, three six-cylinders in the 320i, 323i and 328i, and a four-cylinder diesel in the 320d. These were joined by a sixth engine for the 316i, announced at the Amsterdam Show in February 1999.

Every engine in the new range had chain-driven camshafts, but four-valve configurations were not yet universal: the 316i and 318i engines still relied on two valves per cylinder. Both petrol and diesel types had roller-type drag arms in the valvetrain to minimize friction losses, and the exhaust emissions of every engine met the EU3 standards scheduled for European introduction in 2000. The petrol engines had a new and extraordinarily sophisticated management

328i (1997 on) and 328Ci (1999 on)

As for 318i, except:

Engine

Cylinders	Six
Bore × stroke	84 × 84mm
Capacity	2793cc
Valves	Four per cylinder
Timing	Chain-driven twin ohc and Double-VANOS variable valve timing
Compression ratio	10.2:1
Engine management	BMW DMS 46 system
Exhaust	Fitted with twin catalytic converters
Max. power	193bhp at 5500rpm
Max torque	207lb/ft at 3500rpm

Transmission

Gearbox	Five-speed close-ratio manual	
Ratios	Normal	five-speed overdrive automatic
First	4.21:1	3.67:1
Second	2.49:1	2.00:1
Third	1.66:1	1.41:1
Fourth	1.24:1	1.00:1
Fifth	1.00:1	0.74:1
Final drive	2.93:1	3.07:1

Wheels and Tyres

7J × 16 wheels with 205/55 R 16 tyres

Dimensions

Track	Front 1471mm (57.91in) Rear 1478mm (58.19in)
Unladen weight	1,470–1,505kg (3,241–3,318lb), depending on specification

system called DMS 46, which had been developed by BMW in conjunction with Siemens. This system even controlled the

coolant temperature, as on BMW's V8 engines, to maintain optimum operating conditions for good fuel economy.

Once again, the performance hierarchy was quite clear, but what was noticeable this time was the excellent performance of the new four-cylinder diesel engine in the 320d. Right at the bottom of the range was the 105bhp 316i, which promised 0–62mph in 12.4 seconds and a top speed of 124mph (200km/h). Next up was the 118bhp 318i, offering 0–62mph in 10.4 seconds and a maximum speed of 128mph (206km/h). The 136bhp 320d engine, meanwhile, promised the same top speed but with a 0–62mph time of just 9.9 seconds. As for the six-cylinders, the 150bhp 320i could hit 62mph in the same 9.9 seconds and run on to 136mph (219km/h), the 170bhp 323i gave 144mph (232km/h) and 0–62mph in 8 seconds, while the top-of-the-range 328i reached 62mph from rest in 7 seconds dead and went on to 149mph (240km/h).

Confusingly, the 316i and 318i models were both powered by 1895cc M43 engines. The difference lay in the engine's state of tune. Both versions of the engine brought improved torque response in the low and medium speed ranges, as compared to earlier types with the same capacity. This was achieved largely by the use of BMW's inlet manifold with variable-length tracts (known as ICIM), and partly by the new DMS 46 engine management system. The M43 had also been designed with twin counter-rotating balancer-shafts below the crankshaft that smoothed out the second-order mass forces to give a level of running refinement comparable to that of a V6 engine. The 8kg (18lb) of extra weight which these shafts brought was offset by a new plastic inlet manifold and by the removal of unwanted sound insulation – for the new engine reduced interior noise by as much as 10dBA.

The M43 four-cylinder engine powered both 316i and 318i models. This is the 1.9ltr 318i version.

Six-cylinder E46s boasted the Double-VANOS M52 engine.

The two six-cylinders belonged to the M52 family and shared their bore and stroke dimensions with the M52 types in the outgoing 323i and 328i models. They also shared power outputs with the earlier engines, but their torque outputs were very different. Between idling speed and 3,000rpm – the most commonly-used rev range – each engine offered up to 90 per cent of its maximum torque to improve driveability.

This change was mainly attributable to the addition of the Double-VANOS variable valve timing system pioneered on the Evolution versions of the E36 M3, but these

The 2ltr M47 four-cylinder diesel is seen here with its intercooler.

engines also boasted an ICIM variable intake manifold. Twin catalytic converters inside the exhaust manifolds minimized power losses and also improved warm-up time and therefore the effectiveness of the emissions control system. BMW boasted that emissions were good enough to meet the latest Californian LEV (low-emissions vehicle) limits, and that with a few adjustments they could be made to meet the extremely strict ULEV (ultra-low emissions vehicle) limits.

The M47 engine in the 320d, meanwhile, was an intercooled turbocharged four-cylinder diesel with four valves per cylinder. It was BMW's first direct-injection engine, all earlier diesels having used indirect injection because of the system's lower noise levels. Direct injection was nevertheless more fuel-efficient, and that characteristic was boosted in the M47 by the very latest common-rail injection system, with a radial-piston pump to give the necessary high injection pressures. Two-stage injection, with a pilot injection of fuel before the main charge, eliminated the characteristic knock of direct-injection engines so that the M47 was as quiet as BMW's older six-cylinder diesels.

Further advances meant instantaneous cold-starting except in temperatures below freezing, and therefore a virtual end to the brief delay needed while glow-plugs warmed the combustion chambers. Finally, diesel engines traditionally gave good response at low speeds and poor response at high speeds, but BMW had eliminated this by using variable intake geometry on the turbo-charger. This was achieved by adjusting the position of the guide blades which direct the flow of exhaust gas to the turbine, which in turn varied the boost pressure to the engine. As a result, the 320d gave excellent high-speed acceleration in addition to the traditional low-speed torque of a diesel engine.

THE GEARBOXES

At its introduction, the E46 range featured three major types of gearbox. Standard on all models was a five-speed close-ratio manual, with direct-drive top gear. This was the only gearbox available on the 320d, but all three other models could be bought with an automatic alternative, linked by CAN bus to the engine management system for optimum shift smoothness. On the four-cylinder 318i, this was a four-speed type with overdrive top gear, but the six-cylinder models had a five-speed overdrive type. All gearboxes were 'filled for life' – which actually meant that they did not need an oil change until they had covered 94,000 miles, or 150,000km.

The five-speed gearbox came with three different gear sets. While the 318i and 323i models used the same ratios, the 320d gearbox had shorter ratios on all four lower gears to improve acceleration, and the 328i gearbox had shorter first, second and fourth ratios. In all cases, a self-adjusting clutch was fitted, to minimize maintenance. The four-speed automatic gearbox came with AGS, which electronically 'learned' the driver's style and adjusted the gearshift shift points to suit it. The five-speed came with BMW's much-liked Steptronic control system, as seen earlier on the E39 5 Series cars. This consisted of an H-gate, with a traditional automatic gate on one side and a sequential manual selector on the other. Both automatic gearboxes came with Shift-lock (which prevented the gear lever being moved from P or N unless the footbrake was operated) and with Interlock (which prevented the ignition key from being removed unless P had been selected).

THE COUPÉ

The stylish two-door coupé derivative of the E46 3 Series was announced at the Geneva Show in March 1999. With it came the slightly suprising news that the coupé derivatives would have their own badging: instead of carrying the same badges as the saloons, they would have distinctive names

The coupé was the second E46 body style to appear and retained the excellent visual balance of the four-door saloon. Those styling creases along the flanks help to disguise the height of the body sides.

The E46 coupé is seen here in right-hand drive form, with the standard seven-spoke wheels used on less expnsive variants. Despite its close resemblance to the four-door saloon, there are subtle distinguishing touches. Note, for example, the curved inner edges of the front indicator lenses.

The rear end of the coupé models was very similar to the saloon type, but note the fog guard lamps in the rear apron and the distinguishing C in the badge.

incorporating an extra 'C'. Thus, in the initial model release, there were 318Ci, 320Ci, 323Ci and 328Ci versions.

Even though the coupé was readily recognizable as a close relative of the four-door saloon, almost all of its external panels were unique. Even the windscreen was raked a further two degrees to create the right lines and the car was marginally longer because

of an increased overhang at the rear. Particularly noticeable was the special front treatment, where the grille, headlamps and spoiler all differed from their saloon counterparts.

The grille was wider and more rounded – following a trend seen on other BMWs of the time – and its two sections sported broader chrome frames, while the scalloped panel

Refreshing interior colour schemes were unique to the E46 coupés.

Coupé front seats tipped forwards to give access to the rear.

under the headlamps was subtly different from the saloon type. The spoiler, meanwhile, was deeper and embraced a much larger air intake, with circular fog lamps inset into its outer ends. Under the rear bumper, the apron differed yet again, being deeper and incorporating two fog guard lamps.

The general ambience inside the car was very similar to that of the saloons, but the seats were set some 10mm lower to restore

some of the headroom lost to the lower roofline. The door trims were also more stylish, and their extra length allowed the designers to go for more sweeping curves, and to incorporate the door speakers in their own binnacles.

Drivetrains were identical to those in the equivalent saloons, and as overall weights were similar and the rakish body not actually much more aerodynamic, performance of all models was much the same. Never-

As expected, a Touring version of the 3 Series also entered production. The lines remained sporty, despite the third side window and the van-like two-box profile.

Acronyms

Like other modern BMWs, the E46 cars feature a number of sophisticated driving and safety aids. Mainly electronic, these systems are usually identified by acronyms of their English (rather than German) names.

ABS Available on BMWs for many years, ABS is an anti-lock brake system. It operates by using wheel sensors to detect when one wheel is spinning more slowly than the others, as occurs if a wheel locks up under braking. Electronics then pulse the brake on that wheel rapidly, to allow it to regain traction and so perform a useful braking function once again. ABS, originally invented in the early 1970s, is not an acronym for an English name but rather for the German *Anti-Blockier System*. The wheel sensors and electronic circuitry of the ABS system are the foundation on which other traction aids are built.

AGS The Adaptive Gearbox System is an electronically controlled 'intelligent' system which adapts the shift points in the automatic gearbox to suit the driver's style of driving.

AIC Automatic Intermittent Control senses the amount of rain falling on the windscreen and adjusts the wiper speed to suit.

ASC+T These letters stand for Automatic Stability Control and Traction. This is a system which uses the ABS circuitry to detect wheelspin (as may occur under hard acceleration from rest). A spinning wheel is automatically braked so that it can gain traction. ASC+T is really a modern electronic equivalent of the limited-slip differential, but it can prevent wheelspin in situations where a limited-slip differential cannot.

CBC Cornering Brake Control also uses the ABS sensors to prevent oversteer or a slide if the brakes are applied at extremes of traction as, for example, during hard cornering.

CCC The Controlled Converter Clutch limits torque converter slip in the automatic transmissions.

DSC III This is the third-generation version of BMW's Dynamic Stability Control system – hence the 'III'. The system computes the intended course through a corner by measuring steering input, yaw angle and transverse acceleration, and from the result it decides whether the car is going to drift off the desired trajectory. To redress the situation, it reduces engine power and applies the brakes to individual wheels until stability is restored.

EWS III A rolling-code immobilizer with a choice of over 100 billion possible codes, to make things difficult for car thieves.

ICIM Individually-Controlled Intake Manifold was first introduced on larger cars in the BMW range, and is a system in which the engine control unit varies the effective length of each inlet tract in order to maximize torque.

ITS Inflatable Tubular Structure is BMW's name for the side airbag at head height.

OBD On Board Diagnosis is a system by which the emissions of the engine can be monitored by simply plugging a reader into the OBD socket.

PDC Park Distance Control is fitted into the rear bumper, and uses sensors which operate an audible driver warning that the car is being reversed close to an obstruction.

SII BMW's Service Interval Indicator is a system of dashboard lights which inform the driver of the mileage to the next oil change.

SRS Supplementary Restraint System is the industry name for airbags.

TPC Tyre Pressure Control monitors air pressure in each tyre, and illuminates a yellow warning message ('check tyre pressure') on the dashboard if it detects a loss of pressure. A more sudden deflation results in a red warning message, reading 'puncture'.

---

theless, there were suspension revisions to suit the car's more sporting nature. The car sat 15mm lower on its wheels, and those wheels were wider 7J items with a 16in diameter instead of the 15in standard on saloons. This meant, of course, that lower-profile tyres were standard. The basic wheels were seven-spoke alloys of the same design as the saloons – although, of course, an inch larger in diameter. At extra cost, these could be changed for two-piece cross-spoke alloys, new star-pattern alloys with split spokes (giving ten spokes in all), or 17in eight-spoke alloys, each spoke being doubled to give a total of sixteen spokes.

Production Totals

All models included in these figures were saloons. The figures include CKD and SKD production, and are worldwide totals.

1997	633
1998	198,086

---

8 Aftermarket Tuned 3 Series BMWs

The oldest and best-known of the companies which worked on the 3 Series BMWs was Alpina, based in Buchloe, some sixty miles from BMW headquarters in Munich. Founded in 1965 by Burkard Bovensiepen, the company had established a formidable reputation in Germany, initially as a supplier of speed equipment and later through its own racing team. Although Bovensiepen worked on other marques in the very early days, his company quickly began to specialize in BMWs and established a very close relationship with the manufacturer. Team Alpina also prepared the BMW CSL coupé which won the 1977 European Touring Car Championship.

Alpina remains an independent concern, although its status is really that of an officially approved modifier of BMWs. The company is registered in Germany as a motor manufacturer, and Bovensiepen himself notoriously vents his anger on those who describe his company as a conversion or tuning outfit! Today's Alpina BMWs are very much more than conversions: they are BMW cars which have been completely re-engineered to give high performance with safety. Demand has led to the addition of cosmetic and luxury features, but an Alpina BMW is still highly respected as the ultimate high-performance machine.

Left-hand drive Alpina BMWs have always been built at the company's premises in Buchloe, Bavaria. Between 1983 and 1993, right-hand drive cars were built under an exclusive agreement by the BMW dealership Sytner of Nottingham. Alpina has many other outlets around the world – and many Alpina items are available through BMW franchised dealers – but none of these can actually manufacture the cars.

THE ALPINA E21

The first Alpina 3 Series cars were based on the E21 models, and became available during 1976. They were known simply as the 320 Alpina and 320i Alpina, and were based on the standard production models which their names suggested. By 1978, a 333i Alpina was also available, based on the six-cylinder E21, and by the end of the E21 production run it was also possible to buy a 330i model.

In this period, the typical Alpina 3 Series had a five-speed close-ratio Getrag gearbox with dog's-leg first in place of the factory-issue four-speed. The rear axle was equipped with a 75 per cent limited-slip differential. Suspension modifications included stiffer springs, matched Bilstein gas dampers, uprated anti-roll bars and a lowered front ride height. Cross-drilled brake discs were available, but were an optional extra, as was an enlarged fuel tank.

Wheels were invariably multi-spoke types to an Alpina design manufactured by BBS. Early cars had 13in wheels, with 5.5in rims at the front and 6.5in rims at the rear, run-

Alpina was always the foremost name among high-performance 3 Series specialists. These are two of its E36 models: on the left is a B6 2.8, and on the right a B2.5 Coupé. Note the multi-spoked alloy wheels which were an Alpina trademark. Neither of these UK-market cars has side-stripes, which were not much liked in Britain.

ning on 70-section Pirelli tyres. By 1977, however, 15in wheels with 6.5in rims at the front and 7.5in rims at the rear were the favoured types. These ran on the latest ultra-low-profile Pirelli P7 tyres, in 195/50VR15 size for the front wheels and 205/50VR15 for the rears. The P7 tyres gave astounding levels of grip in the dry, but were well-known for letting go suddenly on a wet surface.

E21 Alpina cars had a deep front spoiler, with air scoops designed to direct air onto the front brakes. Invariably applied was a 'deco-set' of stripes for the front spoiler, the sides and the boot lid. These were an Alpina trademark which had been introduced on

the 2002 models, and prominently displayed the Alpina name. Interiors featured front bucket seats made by Schee, and the upholstery was all in a rather garish fabric with blue and green stripes. Standard fit was a four-spoke Momo leather-rimmed steering wheel bearing the Alpina name, and optional was a rosewood gear-knob with the Alpina emblem. The speedometer and rev counter were normally replaced by Alpina-badged items.

The heart of every Alpina BMW has, of course, always been its engine, and the engines in the E12 models were no exception. The basic four-cylinder 2ltr engine, which came from BMW with 109bhp and a

The Alpina Emblem

The blue and red Alpina emblem is instantly recognizable, but what it actually symbolizes is less well-known. In fact, the left-hand side of the emblem shows a pair of induction pipes, and the right-hand side a crankshaft.

The Alpina emblem features the intake pipes from a fuel system, and a crankshaft.

single Solex carburettor, was available in three states of tune from Alpina during 1976. The first stage brought 125bhp; the second stage added twin Solex 45 DDH carburettors and a 300-degree camshaft to give 150bhp at 6900rpm; and the third stage added Kugelfischer fuel injection to give 160bhp at 6400rpm. These engine modifications had their basis in the work which Alpina had done on the 2ltr 'four' for the earlier 2002 models. In each case, the cylinder head was modified, and new light-weight Mahle pistons raised the compression ratio.

It is no simple matter to establish definitive performance figures for these E21 Alpinas, because they were built very much as individual cars to meet the wishes of individual customers. Alpina had not yet established itself fully as a manufacturer, and offered a variety of different options rather than the standardized packages of later years. Thus, the 320 Alpina tested in

Britain by *Car* magazine in its September 1976 issue retained its four-speed gearbox allied to a taller final drive. Not surprisingly, perhaps, bottom-end performance seemed a little disappointing, but the 150bhp twin-Solex engine delivered 60mph (100km/h) from rest in under seven seconds and a maximum of 130mph (210km/h).

Just over a year later, *Road and Track* in America tested a 160bhp 320i with the standard 3.64:1 final drive and found it took 8.5 seconds to reach 60mph and ran out of steam at 119mph (191km/h). This car, assembled in California by a company then hoping to represent Alpina in the USA, did not sport any emissions-control equipment, so it is hard to understand why it should have been so much slower than the less powerful British car.

When the standard 320 switched to a 122bhp six-cylinder engine in 1977, Alpina embarked on a different course. By 1978, the company was offering a 333i Alpina, which was similar in all respects to its earlier 320 models, except that it had the big-block six-cylinder engine used in the BMW 633Csi coupé. With the standard 3210cc swept volume, but much-modified by Alpina, this promised 220bhp at 6000rpm and 228lb/ft of torque at 4500rpm. The familiar Getrag close-ratio five-speed gearbox was allied to a 3.36:1 final drive and a 75 per cent limited-slip differential. To improve weight distribution (and also to make more room for the much bigger engine under the bonnet), the battery was moved to the boot.

Another Californian company hoping to represent Alpina in the USA put one of these together for test purposes. The car was lent to *Road and Track*, who published a test report in their November 1978 issue. Once again, the engine carried no emissions-control equipment. The 0–60mph time of 7 seconds which the magazine recorded was certainly promising, but the top speed of 129mph (208km/h) a big disappointment.

The next stage in Alpina's development was ushered in by Dr Fritz Indra, who was then in charge of engine development. Alpina was coming up against two major problems. The first was that the modification packages which the company produced might not always give the expected performance gains when fitted by non-specialists. The second was that regulations governing such issues as exhaust emissions, safety and noise already differed from one country to the next, and it was clear that their complexity and diversity were likely to increase. So Indra proposed that Alpina should stop offering packages which suited some countries but not others, and instead should offer complete cars to a standardized specification.

This idea gained Bovensiepen's full support, and during 1977 Alpina embarked on a major expansion programme at Buchloe, building a factory extension which would boost the company's annual production capacity to 250 cars. A standardized specification was drawn up to suit 3, 5 and 6 Series models from BMW. The 3 Series car was to be known as a B6 2.8, and the prototype example was ready for final testing along with the other standardized Alpina models by May 1978. Later that year, the B6 2.8 went on sale.

The B6 2.8 was once again based on an E21 model and had an Alpina-tuned version of BMW's 2788cc big-block six-cylinder engine. With a modified cylinder head, new Mahle pistons, a compression ratio raised from the standard 9:1 to 9.5:1, Solex DL mechanical fuel injection and Hartig computerized ignition, the engine delivered 210bhp at 6100rpm and 206lb/ft at 5000rpm. It drove through the familiar Getrag close-ratio five-speed gearbox to a final drive which had been raised to 3.24:1. Alpina claimed an astonishing maximum speed of 143mph (230km/h), with 0–60mph in 6.9 seconds.

Like earlier Alpina E21s, the B6 2.8 had a deep front air dam, body striping tapes and multi-spoke 15in alloy wheels. There were 6in rims on the front and 7in rims at the rear, with Pirelli P7 tyres. The suspension had been uprated with the tried and tested combination of stiffer springs and Bilstein gas dampers, but the B6 2.8 also had a pair of additional rear radius arms to improve wheel location and tame the E21's tendency to rear-end breakaway. There was also an adjustable anti-roll bar at the back, while the front disc brakes were cross-drilled as standard. The battery had once again migrated to the boot and the auxiliary fuel tank was now a standard feature. Scheel front buckets seats and Alpina's green and blue striped upholstery were standard; the speedometer and rev counter carried Alpina logos; and the steering wheel was a four-spoke Momo. Lastly, a black rubber spoiler had been added to the trailing edge of the boot lid to give some extra down-force at the high speeds of which the car was capable.

Alpina also developed an entry-level version of their E21 3 Series, based on the 323i. A prototype was built in 1979, and the C1 2.3 was introduced in 1980. Much less radical than the B6 2.8, it nevertheless featured all the familiar Alpina spoilers, stripes and interior addenda, together with suspension and braking upgrades. The engine retained the capacity of the standard 323i unit, but had been developed to give 170bhp at 5800rpm and 166lb/ft at 4500rpm.

THE ALPINA E30

BMW introduced the E30 3 Series cars to replace the first-generation E21s in 1982, and it took Alpina a while to develop its own E30 variants. However, a B6 2.8 became available during 1983, and C1 2.3 models in early 1984, both using the engines which had been developed for the E21 cars which first carried those names. The B6 2.8, which had broadly similar performance to the earlier car of the same name, was followed in 1986 by the astonishing and rare B6 3.5S, based on the then-new E30 M3.

Meanwhile, in 1983, Sytner BMW in Nottingham signed an exclusive contract to build Alpina cars with right-hand drive. Thus the first fully-engineered Alpina 3 Series not to have their steering on the left were E30 models. Sytner started in a small way with the C1 2.3, but by early 1985 had actually developed its own car – the C2 – and had started to build examples before the Buchloe factory. The C2 was quickly developed into the C2 2.7, and later became available for the E30 cabriolet and E30 Touring models as well. During this period,

the Getrag close-ratio five-speed gearbox was still recommended, but some cars were built with overdrive five-speed gearboxes and some of the C Series models were even supplied with four-speed ZF automatic transmissions.

Alpina continued to sell add-on packages in this period, although the high-performance engines were only available in complete cars from Buchloe or Nottingham. Thus it was possible to buy for any standard E30 a suspension and wheel kit, which consisted of the Alpina springs, dampers, wheels and tyres. Spoilers, the Momo steering wheel, and the long-range fuel tank could also be bought as add-ons. In Britain the so-called C-pack included all of these items and added body stripes, Alpina badges, and a wooden gear-lever knob.

The typical Alpina E30 still carried body decals until the mid-1980s, but from about 1986 there was something of a reaction to these. They had never been much liked in Britain, and the BMW factory had taken a very different approach with the understatement of its 1984 M5 and 1986 M3 models. Therefore, later Alpina E30s often dispensed with the decals. Early cars still had the blue and green striped upholstery, but the front bucket seats were now made by Recaro and not by Scheel. Suspension modifications once again focused on stiffer springs, although now those at the rear were progressive-rate types. Bilstein gas dampers were still in favour, and the stylish Alpina multi-spoke alloy wheels still distinguished the company's cars at a glance.

However, Alpina E30s had moved up to 16in wheels. These had 7in rims all round, and ran on Pirelli P7 195/50 × 16 tyres. By 1987, the choice had shifted to 7in rims at the front with 8in rims at the rear, and the tyres were Michelin MXW 205/50 × 16 and 225/45 × 16 respectively. Limited-slip differentials were still part of the standard specification, but 25 per cent types were now fitted.

The C1 2.3 model, based on the production 323i, was not as much of a success as Alpina had hoped, and the company was probably quite pleased to drop it when BMW raised the performance stakes by making their top E30 a 171bhp 2.5ltr model in 1985. This made the 170bhp C1 2.3 an expensive irrelevance.

Motor tried a Sytner-built C1 2.3 in its issue of 9 June 1984, and came away from the experience very disappointed. The car had the standard five-speed overdrive gearbox rather than the close-ratio Getrag, which might have explained some of this, but with a compression ratio raised to 10:1 (9.8:1 was standard) and 170bhp at 6000rpm, the car recorded a 0–60mph standing-start time of 7 seconds. This was half a second faster than the magazine's earlier road-test 323i, but a best speed of just over 132mph (210km/h) suggested that this expensive bespoke car could not offer very much that was not already available from the standard 128mph 323i. The *Motor* testers also complained that the engine was very 'cammy', not getting into its stride until well up the rev band.

The Sytner-developed C2 was a much more interesting car. Introduced early in 1985, it was based on a 323i but had a 2.5ltr engine. This had been developed with great economy, by mating the 84mm-bore block of the 2.7ltr 'eta' engine (seen in the 325e and 525e) with the short-stroke crankshaft of the 323i. This gave a swept volume of 2492cc, and to it was added the Alpina-developed cylinder head of the C1 2.3. The results were 185bhp at 6100rpm and 179lb/ft of torque at 5000rpm.

With the overdrive five-speed gearbox and a 3.45:1 final drive, the C2 tested by *Autocar* for its issue of 20 February 1985 hit 60mph in 7.6 seconds and ran on to 142mph (228km/h). A later test of a car with the Getrag close-ratio gearbox and 3.25:1 final drive proved abortive because of poor weather, but Sytner claimed believable figures of 0–60mph in 6.6 seconds and a maximum of 134mph (216km/h).

The C2 2.7 was an altogether more impressive piece of machinery. This time, the whole bottom end of the 2693cc 'eta' engine was used, together with the existing Alpina-developed cylinder head. On a 10.2:1 compression, the engine developed 210bhp at 5800rpm and had a maximum torque of 213lb/ft at 4500rpm. *Autocar* tested a C2 2.7 with overdrive gearbox in its issue of 12 March 1986, and reported acceleration of 0–60mph in 6.6 seconds. However, the car was unable to match the claimed 144mph (232km/h) maximum on its 3.46:1 final drive. For better acceleration but a lower maximum, the C2 2.7 could be had with lower gearing of 3.64:1 and a Getrag close-ratio gearbox. The ZF four-speed automatic was also an option, with a 4.1:1 final drive. When *Autocar* tested an automatic C2 2.7 in its issue of 17 August 1988, the results were 131mph (211km/h), as against a claimed 140mph, and a 0–60mph time of 7.3 seconds.

The most exciting of Alpina's E30 variants – and the rarest – was undoubtedly the B6 3.5S. This was announced towards the end of 1988, and was available both with and without an exhaust catalyst. The car was based on an M3, and was therefore only ever available with left-hand drive. To create a B6 3.5S, Alpina removed the M3's four-cylinder, four-valve engine, and replaced it by their own uprated edition of the BMW 3453cc big-block six. This engine had already appeared in the Alpina B10 versions of larger BMWs. Without the restriction of a catalytic converter, it delivered 260bhp at 6000rpm and 236lb/ft at 4000rpm. The catalyst-equipped version was only slightly less powerful, with 254bhp. Power-to-weight ratio of the complete car was thus staggering, at over 200bhp per ton.

This engine drove through the standard M3 gearbox (a Getrag close-ratio five-speed similar to the one favoured by Alpina in other E30s) to a final drive which had been raised to 2.79:1. A 25 per cent limited-slip differential was also part of the package. Yet almost nothing else was changed on the car. The stiffer front springs used on air-conditioned M3s were specified to help offset the extra weight of the six-cylinder engine, and Alpina multi-spoke alloy wheels were fitted. These had a 16in diameter and 8in rims, and wore 225/45 VR 16 Michelin MXX tyres. Alpina's claims for this brutal machine were 156mph (251km/h) and 0–60mph in 6.5 seconds.

THE ALPINA E36

The faithful B6 2.8 became the first E36 Alpina in 1991, carrying over its engine from the E30 model of the same name. With 240bhp at 6000rpm and 213lb/ft at 4700rpm, this car offered a governed 156mph (250km/h) top speed (and was capable of more without the limiter) and 0–60mph in a

shade over 6 seconds. However, it was superseded during 1993 by the B3, with a 3ltr engine developed from the M3's six-cylinder. This in turn was superseded by a B3 3.2 in 1996, and supplemented by the storming V8-powered B8 4.6 in 1995.

Alpina 3 Series cars of this period still retained many of the company's characteristics, such as the deep front air dam and multi-spoke alloy wheels, and even side stripes were still available for anybody who wanted them. Seats were normally upholstered in supple leather, however. The buying public of the E36, educated by BMW's own Motorsport cars to expect performance with discretion, wanted nothing less.

Stiffer springs, lower ride height and Bilstein gas dampers were all part of the Alpina magic as it affected the E36 cars. Wheels in this period had a 17in diameter. The B3s had 9in rims front and rear with Michelin MXX3 265/35 ZR 17 tyres, but the later 3.2ltr and 4.6ltr cars had Michelin Pilot SX tyres with a narrower 235/40 ZR 17 size on the front wheels with 8in rims to give sharper handling. The 235/35 size were retained on 9in rims for the rear wheels of these models.

The B3 3.2 was based on the E36 and could be had as a coupé, as a four-door saloon (seen here) . . .

. . . as a cabriolet . . .

. . . or as a Touring estate. These German-market cars all have the Alpina side-stripes.

The engine of the B3 was based on the 2990cc iron-block motor of the early E36 M3. In Alpina-tuned form, it delivered a surprisingly low 241bhp at 5700rpm, which nevertheless endowed the car with a 0–62mph (0–100km/h) time of 6.6 seconds and a top speed governed to 156mph. Bored and stroked to 3.2 litres for the B3 3.2 in 1996, this engine had 257bhp at 5800rpm and 243lb/ft at 4200rpm. These figures were substantially below those of BMW's own M3 Evo, but Alpina argued that their car offered a different, more involving driving experience.

Be that as it may, Alpina were obliged to find a market niche for the B3 3.2 where they were not up against the M3 Evo, so the model was offered as a Touring, the high-performance estate market being one which BMW's Motorsport division had decided to avoid.

Where Alpina did score over the BMW Motorsport E36 offerings, however, was with its B8 4.6. The 4ltr V8 engine available in the 8 Series coupés and in the saloons of the 5 and 7 Series ranges gave 286bhp in standard trim, and Alpina developed this primarily for their own versions of the bigger

The B8 4.6 models were available only with left-hand drive. This is the four-door saloon . . .

. . . this is the cabriolet . . .

. . . and this is the Touring version. A coupé was also available.

Switchtronic

At the end of 1994, Alpina introduced a new gear-changing option – Switchtronic – which brought Formula 1-like finger-tip control to the ZF automatic transmissions used in BMWs, making it unnecessary for the driver to take a hand off the wheel to change gear. It was available on all Alpina models, including its E36 cars.

The first versions of Switchtronic were operated by pressure-sensitive thumb-pads located just outboard of the steering wheel hub on the wheel's two horizontal spokes. Later versions had more accessible switches behind the spokes. On both versions, the switch on the left gave immediate down-shifts, while that on the right gave immediate up-shifts – subject, of course, to the consent of an electronic control unit.

On the transmission tunnel, the standard shift lever and gate of the automatic transmission remained in place. Normal operation was available when the mode selector was in 'E', although in place of the Economy mode which this usually indicated was a sporting mode. Position 'S' on the selector brought the Switchtronic into operation. The gear selected was shown in a digital display at the bottom of the standard instrument binnacle.

The electronic control unit inhibited down-shifts which would over-speed the engine, and automatically changed up a gear just before the red line was reached. Kick-down was available in the normal way, and the transmission would normally offer a second-speed start unless over-ridden.

BMWs. However, squeezing it into the engine bay of the E36 produced an astonishing machine which upheld the Alpina performance tradition in the face of severe competition from the factory's own products.

The stretch to 4.6 litres was achieved by boring the engine out from 89mm to 93mm, and fitting a new crankshaft with an 85mm stroke in place of the standard 80mm type. With additional work on the cylinder heads and engine management system, Alpina took power up to 328bhp at 5700rpm and torque to 347lb/ft at 3900rpm. With BMW's six-speed close-ratio and overdrive gearbox allied to a 2.79:1 final drive, the unrestricted B8 4.6 would reach 174mph (280km/h) and could hit 60mph from rest in just 5.5 seconds. This was undoubtedly impressive, and it offered a maximum which even the M3 Evo could not match. However, it is worth remembering that the factory's own car was restricted to 156mph in accordance with the gentleman's agreement among German motor manufacturers; the fact that Alpina had broken ranks and brought to market an unrestricted car indi-

cated a measure of desperation in the company's attempts to better the BMW Motorsport division's offerings.

OTHER TUNED E30 MODELS

The aftermarket tuners really got into their stride during the production of the E30 models. The market conditions were right, with a buoyant world economy for most of the 1980s and a boom at the end of the decade. More buyers were willing and able to spend money on their cars – and the car to have was a BMW E30. It would be impossible to list every single aftermarket conversion which was available, but it is possible to give a flavour of the period with a few examples.

Interstate

During 1985, Interstate of Delft in the Netherlands introduced a turbocharged conversion for the 323i. The engine was bored out to give a swept volume of 2550cc, and the exhaust manifold was modified to

Hartge's 2.7ltr high-performance engine is seen here in an E30. Note also the chromed brace bars, which add rigidity to the bodyshell.

Subtly different in appearance, this is one of Hartge's own alloy wheels.

The Hartge H35 conversion put a tuned version of BMW's 3.5ltr six-cylinder engine into an E30 3 Series.

Typical of Hartge visually is this H27 conversion of an E30.

Hartge's H27 engine brought 220bhp to a 325 or 325iX of the E30 range.

Most of the 3 Series BMWs tuned for high performance by aftermarket specialists were developed for European conditions. During the 1980s there was still a wide gap between US emissions regulations and those in Europe, with the effect that most of the tuned cars were not legal for use in the USA. Several small US companies tried to adapt these tuned cars to meet local regulations, but the work involved was costly and reduced the intended performance of the cars. As a result, tuned 3 Series were not the big business in the USA that they were in Europe.

Since 1989, when catalytic converters have been mandatory on all new cars sold in Europe, European and US requirements have been much closer. However, the American homologation requirements insist that powertrains are put through a series of very expensive tests before they can go on sale. Few European companies have the resources to do this, or expect the likely sales to justify the cost.

incorporate a turbocharger. An intercooler was also fitted. Interstate claimed 210bhp at 5500rpm and 222lb/ft at 4000rpm, giving 0–60mph in just under 7 seconds and a maximum of 137mph (220km/h). Other modifications included lowered suspension with Koni adjustable dampers, and BBS spoked alloy wheels with 8J × 16 on the front and 9J × 16 on the rear; tyres were 205/55 VR 16 and 225/50 VR 16 respectively. Also available was a body kit of spoilers and four rectangular headlamps.

MK Motorsport

MK Motorsport in Germany offered an E30 conversion which was similar to the Alpina C2, but could be cheaper because its elements were obtainable individually rather than as a complete package. Based on the 'eta' 2.7ltr engine, the MK Motorsport 2.7 had a big-valve cylinder head with a special camshaft, and delivered a claimed 210bhp at 5700rpm. The company recommended adding a limited-slip differential. A bodykit of spoilers was available, as well as the company's own design of multi-spoke alloy wheels, with Michelin TRX 220/45 VR 390 tyres. Additional instruments and interior cosmetic changes could also be had.

Hartge

From Hartge of Beckingen came the H35 conversion, which was delivered as a

AC Schnitzer had a long-standing relationship with BMW and had prepared many of the factory's own racing 3 Series. Yet it was not until the mid-1990s that Schnitzer accessories were given official blessing and became available through BMW dealerships. This E36 shows off a typical selection of alloy wheels and other body addenda.

Schnitzer's body addenda, alloy wheels and side stripes could give the E36 Compact a more aggressive appearance . . .

. . . and an alternative Schnitzer vision of the model is seen here.

Schnitzer accessories were also available to enhance the E36 Touring. This car is actually a Schnitzer S3 3.2, with performance upgrades as well as cosmetic addenda.

Schnitzer's CLS II was based on the E36 Coupé.

complete car in the Alpina tradition rather than as a series of optional packages. This car used the big 3453cc six-cylinder engine, reworked by Hartge with polished heads, a balanced bottom end and Mahle pistons to give 260bhp at 5900rpm and 257lb/ft at 4000rpm. The gearbox was a close-ratio

Getrag type with dog's-leg first gear, and other elements of the drivetrain and rear axle were borrowed from the 635CSi. The bodyshell was stiffened, the brakes uprated, and the tyres were 225/50 VR 16s on 7.5in rims at the front, with 245/45 VR 16s on 8in rims at the rear.

Alpina's early offerings on the E46 saloon continued to feature their characteristic side stripes and multi-spoke alloy wheels. Just visible in this picture is the discreet rear spoiler.

Schnitzer, too, got to work on the E46 Coupé, and this was the very pleasing result.

Hartge's early offerings for the E46 included these stylish multi-spoke alloy wheels.

Hamann quickly got in on the act with some stylish addenda for the E46 saloons.

Hartge claimed a top speed of 150mph (241km/h), and when the British magazine *Fast Lane* tested an H35 for its February 1988 issue, the 0–60mph time of 6.1 seconds actually bettered the manufacturer's claim. Also available from Hartge (although not legal in Germany) was an E30 equipped with the four-valve Motorsport version of the 3.5ltr engine, as used in the M1 coupé. This was claimed to give over 170mph (274km/h).

OTHER TUNED E36 MODELS

The 1990s saw the rise of several new tuning companies specializing in BMWs. Established companies such as AC Schnitzer and Hartge continued to build their highly-respected conversions, and styling accessories for the E36 became big business. Even the recession of the early 1990s did not have any lasting effects.

Large numbers of these converted E36 cars were built to individual customer order, so there is little point in giving an exhaustive account of each one here. However, once again it is worth giving a flavour of what was made available for the E36 models.

Some of the most exciting work was done on the E36 Compact after its introduction in 1994, because this car offered all the under-bonnet space of the regular E36 but was smaller, lighter and potentially more agile. Racing Dynamics in Italy created what was possibly the ultimate Compact, called the K55 and fitted with a 427bhp version of BMW's 5486cc V12 engine. This achieved 0–62mph times of 4.5 seconds and a top speed of 190mph (306km/h).

Other specialists wrung more out of the M3, examples being Hartge, Schnitzer (with the S3 Sport CSL) and Iding Power in Japan (with the 330bhp M3 S-III). At the bottom of the range, Torque Developments wrought magic on the 316i, and Van Aaken improved the performance of the diesel 325tds. Hamann and Mosselman continued to work with turbochargers, while Hartge offered a variety of engine upgrades, such as a 2.3ltr engine in the 318ti and a 2.1ltr H3 2.1S Compact.

There was a positively bewildering array of styling accessories available for the E36. The main names, in alphabetical order, were Evolution 2 Motorsport, Hamann, Hartge, Iding Power, Kelleners, Kerscher Tuning, Lorenz, Opus, Racing Dynamics, Rieger Tuning, AC Schnitzer and Zeemax.

THE E46 AND AFTERMARKET SPECIALISTS

As this book went to press, the first tuned E46 models were beginning to appear in Germany, and the first kits of styling accessories were being brought to market. There can be little doubt that the E46 models will once again attract many aftermarket specialists, or that the results will once again give spectacular and stunningly quick 3 Series variants to those who are prepared to pay the not inconsiderable cost of a conversion.

9 The 3 Series in Competition

BMW had done extraordinarily well on the race-tracks during the early 1970s with the 2002 and its turbocharged derivative, and so the company had a difficult act to follow when it introduced the new E21 3 Series cars to competition work. Nevertheless, the first racing E21s were out as early as 1976, when Eggenberger fielded a 220bhp four-cylinder 320i, and Bo-Christer Emanuelson won the Swedish Track Championship with his 320 a year later.

THE E21s IN COMPETITION

However, the works racers did not appear until 1977, when BMW announced the formation of a new Junior Team. Its drivers were the German Manfred Winkelhock, the Swiss Marc Surer, and Eddie Cheever from the USA, and its cars were specially prepared versions of the 320i. At their heart was the four-valve version of the 2ltr four-cylinder engine which had originally been developed

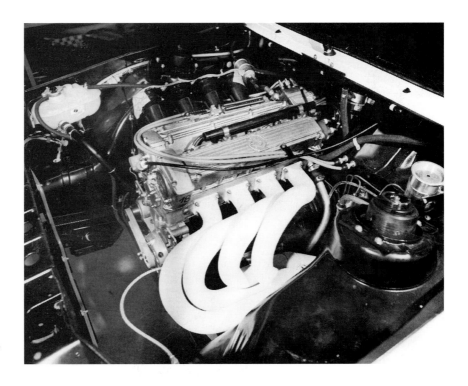

The four-valve 2ltr engine in the racing E21s was essentially BMW's Formula 2 unit. Note how it sits further back than the standard engine.

During 1977, the BMW Junior Team ran E21 320s with 300bhp engines.

Now preserved in the BMW Museum is one of the Junior Team's Group 5 E21 320 cars. Note the huge front spoiler and wide wings. The descriptive sign on the left notes that this car had 300bhp (220kW).

by the Motorsport division for Formula 2 single-seater racing. This engine, the brainchild of Motorsport's Paul Rosche, would be central to the E21's competition career. As first introduced in the E21s, it developed around 305bhp, but this figure crept up as further experience with the engine in its new home enabled the Motorsport engineers to extend its performance envelope.

The E21 racers never did become a major force in international competition, largely because at World Championship level they were pitted against the Porsche Turbos. Nevertheless, during 1977 the F2-engined cars certainly made their mark on touring car events. The Junior Team achieved no fewer than eight victories in that year's German Touring Car Championship and, in the European Touring Car Championship, driver Hans Stuck won a notable victory at Diepholz after ramming a pylon and damaging his car's radiator. For 1978, a new Division 5 for 2ltr cars was opened in the World Manufacturers' Championship, and BMW fielded five 'national' teams, based in Austria, Belgium, Italy, Sweden and Switzerland. It was a strategy which paid off, because the Division 5 title fell to BMW.

However, for 1979, BMW's own competitions activity focused on the special Procar series for the new mid-engined M1, and it was left to private teams to seek glory on the tracks with E21-based cars. This was the era of the turbocharged competitions car, and the team which made the running was Schnitzer. They had developed a turbocharged 320i as early as 1978, when their intention had been to score in the 1.5ltr class. Sleeving down the cylinders of the four-valve F2 engine to 80mm for a swept volume of 1,428cc, Schnitzer had managed to get an astonishing 400bhp out of their car. This was not the first time Schnitzer had gone down this route, as the company

also prepared a 1.4ltr turbocharged 2002 saloon racer for Albrecht Krebs. This time, they were successful, as Harald Ertl won the German Touring Car Championship outright in his 410bhp turbocharged Schnitzer 320i.

Not every turbocharged E21 had the sleeved-down engine, of course, and many were based on the 2ltr Formula 2 Motorsport variant. Although the turbocharged 320i was never as reliable as the naturally-aspirated car, it did deliver the goods on occasion. Hans Stuck, for example, came third in the 1980 German Touring Car Championship with a Schnitzer car. But the best results were achieved in the USA, where David Hobbs and McLaren North America raced a turbocharged 320i in the IMSA series. Their most successful season was in 1979, when Hobbs won four events to give the car third place overall in the series.

THE E30S IN COMPETITION

With the 1982 season came the introduction of new competition regulations that completely changed the face of saloon car racing. Cars eligible for the new Group A events had to be derived from production machines which had sold at least 5,000 examples, and this automatically excluded the highly-specialized turbocharged 320i models which had brought the E21 range its main competition successes. So BMW Motorsport switched the focus of its activity to racers derived from the E28 5 Series saloons and the big E24 6 Series coupés.

When the E30 second-generation 3 Series cars were announced in 1982, the word soon spread within racing circles that BMW were planning a 'homologation special' derivative of the car, and so the private teams held back from using the new model for a time. An exception, however, was Team Linder, who

Bernard Béguin won the 1987 24-hour Snow and Ice event at Chamonix in this 325iX.

entered a 323i driven by Wilfried Vogt in the under-2.5ltr Division II of the 1985 German Touring Car Championship, and won four class victories. The following year, Team Linder switched to the newly-introduced 325i, and with Vogt once again in the driver's seat, came second to Toyota in the Manufacturers' Championship.

However, this was only marking time until the main attraction arrived. The M3 was announced in 1985, and made its racing debut in 1987. BMW decided against financing its own works team, and instead supported the racing activities of a number of private teams. Most notable among these in that first racing season for the M3 was Zakspeed, who had recently defected from Ford. Driving the Zakspeed-prepared M3s were two new teams of drivers. These were a Ladies' Team, made up of Annette

Meeuvissen and Mercedes Steinmetz, and a Junior Team consisting of Marc Hessel and Eric van der Poele. Meanwhile, the established BMW teams fielded drivers including Roberto Ravaglia, Wilfried Vogt, Christian Danner and Markus Oestreich.

From its very first outing, the M3 was a winner, and over the next few years it completely dominated Touring Car racing in Europe. Zakspeed M3s won the 1987 German Touring Car Championship, Wilfried Vogt won the European Championship in a Linder car, with Altfrid Heger second in another M3; overall, M3s took six first places, three seconds and four thirds in the individual rounds that year. The M3 was even successful in rallying, when Bernard Beguin and J-J Lenne won the Tour de Corse in a Prodrive-prepared car. The M3 also won the driver's section of the 1987 World Touring

The E30 M3 racked up an impressive number of victories in Touring Car competition. This is one of the Warsteiner-sponsored cars, seen in action during 1991.

Bernard Béguin is seen here in his E30 M3, on the way to victory in the 1987 Tour de Corse.

Roberto Ravaglia is seen here at the wheel of a Group A M3 during the 1989 German Touring Car Championship.

Car Championship – the only one ever held, the series being withdrawn because of multiple controversies over the regulations. Driving the Schnitzer M3, Roberto Ravaglia claimed no fewer than four outright wins. M3s also won national titles that year in Austria, Finland, France, Holland and Portugal, and carried off the European Hillclimb Championship.

That was just the start of the M3's astonishing competitions career. In 1988, the car won the German Touring Car Championship, and took national titles in France, Germany, Italy and the UK. During 1989 – when the first aerodynamically-modified 'Evolution' M3s raced – Roberto Ravaglia won the German title in a 300bhp Schnitzer car, and Venezuelan-born Johnny Cecotto carried off the Italian equivalent in his BMW Italia car. M3s won more national Touring Car titles in Belgium, Finland, France,

Holland, Spain, Sweden and Yugoslavia. François Dosières took the Touring Car category of the European Hillclimb Championship, and the Belgian Marc Duez successfully campaigned a rallying M3. Prepared in Britain by Prodrive, the Duez car was the highest-placed two-wheel drive car in the 1989 Monte Carlo Rally, and came eighth overall in that event. In partnership with Alain Lopes, Duez also won the Belgian Group A Rally Championship.

The list continued through 1990. That year, BMW increased the engine capacity of the racing machines to just under 2.5ltr, a change which was reflected in the 'homologation special' Sport Evolution. The racers, however, had a rather different engine from the production cars, with a larger 95.5mm bore and a swept volume of 2493cc instead of 2467cc. Roberto Ravaglia won the Italian Touring Car Championship for

The E30 M3 was raced on BMW's behalf by a number of professional teams, and went on to become the most successful Touring Car racer of its day.

Specifications of the E30 M3 Racers

So what was special about this incredibly successful car? As is the case with all competition cars, the racing M3's specification changed not only from year to year, but also from race to race as the teams which prepared the cars found new ways of extracting more power or obtaining better grip. However, it is possible to give some idea of how the cars differed from production versions by looking at typical racing specifications over the five years which formed the core of the M3's racing career.

Although the Group A regulations demanded cars which were closely similar in many respects to the production versions, there were many differences. All the racers, for example, had a strong internal rollcage – and it had been the need for this which had dictated the modified shape of the M3's bodyshell compared to the standard two-door E30 type. Weight was saved wherever possible, and the typical racing weight for an M3 was 960kg (2,117lb). The fuel tank was also much enlarged, to contain 110ltr (24.2gal) of petrol, and featured the typical racing 'bag' inside a foam-lined safety structure made of Kevlar and nylon-reinforced synthetic rubbers.

The cars sat lower on their suspension by as much as 40mm (1.6in), which of course reduced aerodynamic drag at high speeds. Suspension components and hubs were reinforced to withstand

A racing M3 (right) is seen here compared to the road-going car. Note the front suspension brace behind the engine on the racer. The competition M3s normally had just one windscreen wiper, as seen here.

the rigours of the track, and there were bigger brake discs – typically cross-drilled types made by Brembo – with four-piston calipers. In the 1991 German Touring Car Championship, the M3s ran with an ABS system specially developed for the purpose by BMW in conjunction with brake manufacturers Alfred Teves.

Although the low-profile rubber on production cars was quite radical for street use at the time – the first cars had 15in wheels but Evolution versions had 16in types – the racing machines were differently shod. Common in the early days were three-piece modular 17in wheels with 9in rims, running on 245 × 610 tyres. However, some teams preferred 16in wheels with 235/590 × 16 tyres, and in the later stages of the M3's racing career, there were cars equipped with 16in wheels at the front and 17in types at the rear.

the fifth consecutive year in his BMW Italia M3, and there were national Touring Car wins in France (Jean-Pierre Malcher), Holland (Cor Enser) and the UK (Frank Sytner). In France, François Chatriot drove his Prodrive-prepared M3 to victory in the national Rally Championship, as well as campaigning a 280bhp Group A 325iX in snow and ice events. Osella prepared the M3

in which Horst Fendrich won the European Hillclimb Championship, and Dutchman Mathias Moosleitner drove an M3 to victory in the Mitropa Rally Cup.

For 1991, BMW Motorsport recruited Marc Surer to co-ordinate competitions activity, but the M3s were still campaigned by familiar teams such as Zakspeed, Schnitzer, Linder and Bigazzi. The European Touring

An early trial outing for the Group N M3.

*One of the Warsteiner
Group N E36 M3s is
seen here during
testing.*

*Tim Harvey drove
this Vic Lee
Motorsport 318iS
to victory in the
1992 British
Touring Car
Championship.*

The M3 GTR competed in German events in 1993. This is Johnny Cecotto's car.

The E36 cars were very successful for BMW in the 1990s, especially in the new 2ltr Super Touring category.

Car Championship fell to Inaki Goiburu, while in Australia it was Tony Longhurst who became national champion. The M3 claimed further national Touring Car titles in Austria (Helmut König), Britain (William Hoy), Holland (Patrick Huisman), Italy (Roberto Ravaglia, for the sixth time), Japan (Roland Ratzenberger), Spain (José-Maria Ponce), Sweden (Per-Gunnar Anderson) and Switzerland (Hansueli Ulrich).

During 1992, some cars were entered for the new Group N category, which demanded cars as close as possible to production standard. But in October that year, some two years after the last production saloons had been built, the E30 M3 was finally withdrawn as a front-line Touring Car racer. It was still a winning car, and its 1992 successes included national titles in Austria, Czechoslovakia, Denmark, Holland, Luxembourg, South Africa and Spain. In addition, Dagmar Suster carried off both track and hillclimb titles in Slovenia in her M3, Dieter Rottenberger became German Hillclimb Champion, and François Dosières won the European Hillclimb Championship for Touring Cars.

THE E36 IN COMPETITION

With a new M3 on the horizon but not yet available, BMW concentrated on Group N events for the first outings of the E36 models during 1992. The racers' choice was the new coupé, which as a two-door model was lighter than the four-door saloons which were the best-sellers in the range. In the German Touring Car Championship, the favourite was the 325i, but in the British Touring Car Championship which was run to Class 2 (under 2ltr) rules, the 318iS was the car of choice. With one of those, prepared by Vic Lee, Tim Harvey won the 1992 British Touring Car Championship.

In 1993, the FIA introduced a new Super Touring 2ltr category in place of Group A, and this ultimately led to the demise of the M3 as a front-line racing machine. BMW fielded the 318i as its championship contender, although M3s did not disappear entirely from the race-tracks. In Germany, the new M3 GTR competed in the new Warsteiner-ADAC-GT-Cup series. With 325bhp, and weighing just 1,300kg (2,867lb), this car was driven successfully by both Kris Nissen and established BMW driver Johnny Cecotto; it was Cecotto who took the new car to victory.

In Austria, it was an M3 driven by Dieter Quester which won the national championship. Xavier Riera took the Spanish Hillclimb Championship, and Vaclav Bervid became a double champion, in Slovakia and Czechoslovakia. Francisco Egozcue took the European Hillclimb Championship in an Osella-prepared car, while the familiar name of François Dosières cropped up again when he won the European Touring Car Hillclimb Championship. There were also Group N M3s, raced by the Warthofer Ladies' Team of Sabine Schmitz and Astrid Grünfelder.

The first appearances of the 318i racers were crowned with success, as Roberto Ravaglia continued his habit of winning the Italian Touring Car Championship, and Jo Winkelhock (brother of Manfred) drove a Schnitzer-prepared car to victory in the British national event. In Holland, Cor Euser took the under-2ltr Touring Car title with a 320i, while Peter Kox claimed the over-2ltr category with an M3.

For 1994, the four-valve 318iS cars took to the tracks, once again campaigned on behalf of BMW by Team Schnitzer. These were entered for Class 2 events, and in mid-season their need of extra spoilers to improve adhesion to the track led to the 'homologation special' 318iS Class 2 four-door saloons

Hotly pursued by a Peugeot racing saloon, one of the works racing E36 coupés is seen in action in the British Touring Car Championship.

Jo Winkelhock is seen here in his championship-winning 318iS during the 1993 British Touring Car Championship.

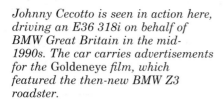

Johnny Cecotto is seen in action here, driving an E36 318i on behalf of BMW Great Britain in the mid-1990s. The car carries advertisements for the Goldeneye film, which featured the then-new BMW Z3 roadster.

which were sold only in Germany. The racing machines had Motorsport-developed S42 engines and six-speed sequential gearboxes, and Johnny Cecotto took one to victory in the German Touring Car Championship.

The mid-1990s were not good times for BMW's efforts in the British Touring Car Championship, and the company did not enter the series in 1997, preferring to concentrate on other events, where it stood more chance. High on the list of priorities was backing for the BMW V12-powered McLaren F1 GTR cars which would run at Le Mans and in other endurance races. Yet the 318iS cars continued to rack up victories elsewhere. In 1995, a 318iS gave Jo Winkelhock the German Super Touring Championship, while Yvan Muller carried off honours in the French Supertourisme series. McLaren provided technical support to Schnitzer during the 1996 season, but the BMWs were beaten into second place in the German Super Touring series by Audi. The news was better in 1997, when Paul Morris took his E36 to victory in the Australian Super Touring Championship.

Team Schnitzer once again represented the factory in European events during 1998, and this time the cars were 320i models driven by Jo Winkelhock and Johnny Cecotto. Yet the big success of this season

came from a most unexpected quarter, when a diesel E36 won the Nurburgring 24-hour race in June. The team of drivers consisted of Christian Menzel, Marc Duez, Andreas Bovensiepen and Hans-Joachim Stuck, and the car was actually a 1996 Warthofer team 320i into which had been transplanted the brand-new four-cylinder turbocharged M47D engine of the E46 models. The car had been developed by Steyr, and adapted to meet the Super Touring regulations by BMW Motorsport. Its engine delivered 220bhp and 295lb/ft of torque.

THE E46 IN COMPETITION

The competition career of the E46 cars had only just begun in earnest as this book went to press, but it seems clear that diesel racers will play a prominent part in it. The Italian MAXteam had already beaten others to the punch by running an E46 320d in endurance racing, and had attracted official backing to the extent that BMW Italia had allowed them to use the livery of the works Super Touring 320i.

BMW Motorsport had also announced the availability of a special 320i-based racer aimed at privateers. Sold in kit form for development and build by the buyer, as the

---

Specifications of an E36 Racer

The 1995 E36 models campaigned by Johnny Cecotto and David Brabham for the Warthofer team in the British Touring Car Championship were based on four-door saloon bodyshells. They featured large rear wings mounted on the boot lid and were powered by Motorsport-developed S42 engines, derived from the 16-valve four-cylinder found in the 318iS coupé and 318ti Compact. However, the 86.5mm bore and 85mm stroke differed from the production dimensions and, at the start of the season, the 1998cc engines were delivering 285bhp at 8500rpm and 184lb/ft at 7000rpm.

The racers had rack-and-pinion steering and ran on forged magnesium 18in multi-spoke wheels with 8in rims. The brakes were 342mm ventilated discs at the front and 283mm ventilated discs at the rear. No ABS was fitted, as it was not permitted under the British Touring Car Championship regulations then in force.

competition E30 M3s had been many years earlier, the car was known as the 320i DTC. Those initials stood for *Deutsche Tourenwagen Challenge* (German Touring Car Challenge), and the car had been prepared to meet the regulations of that series. The basic engine supplied with the car developed around 200bhp – but of course individual tuners were certain to unlock more of its potential during the season to come.

10 Buying a 3 Series BMW

The 3 Series models have always been the affordable BMWs, although that is not the same thing as saying that they are cheap to run. By comparison with other cars of their pretensions and vintage they are, nevertheless, not expensive until they reach very high mileages. Components tend to take a long time to wear out – but when they do, they are likely to be quite expensive to replace. The numbers of tired and scruffy older 3 Series models on the road make clear that the cars are survivors – but also that some are only hanging on to life by habit because their owners cannot afford to maintain them properly.

The name BMW is associated with high-performance machinery, with glamour and with luxury. But not every 3 Series is a high-performance car, not every 3 Series is glamorous, and not every 3 Series is luxurious. These models were, after all, the entry-level BMWs, and the cheapest of them were pretty basic pieces of machinery in spite of their undoubted competence. So buyers who are expecting something special should remember that what is really special about every BMW is the way it is engineered. The other elements associated with the name are carefully fostered by the company's publicity machine, but the reality has not rubbed off on every 3 Series car to be built. Even today's entry-level 3 Series cars are nowhere near as exciting as many people imagine.

Looking beyond the superficial attraction of high performance, leather seats and air conditioning, enthusiasts can see that every single BMW 3 Series has an engineering integrity about it. The cars may have been mass-produced, but they were designed for long working lives, and they were designed to work properly and give their owners satisfaction from the beginning. Thus, the responsiveness and refinement of their engines, the slickness of their gear changes, the reassuring nature of their handling and the sharpness of their steering are qualities to be appreciated in even the most basic versions. Anything on top of that is a bonus.

Regular maintenance is as important for a 3 Series BMW as for any other car, and the cars' reputation for longevity depends upon it.

Many 3 Series enthusiasts are under-standably interested in the value of their cars. This is sometimes perceived as a get-rich-quick attitude, but it is more often down to simple economics: everyone prefers to own something valuable which can be sold in a time of financial emergency. So the question often arises: which are the best 3 Series models to buy for investment?

The answer to that is conditioned by the fact that the 3 Series are by no means rare cars. However, some variants are rarer than others. Rarity itself does not necessarily make for value, of course, and even a pristine E30 324td is never likely to be worth a huge sum of money. So here, the question of glamour does come into the equation: open cars, M3s and professionally-tuned machines (by the likes of Alpina) are always likely to fetch the highest prices. Six-cylinder cars with high equipment levels are always likely to be more valuable than four-cylinder cars with a basic specification, condition being otherwise equal.

Two other pieces of advice are worth passing on before this chapter gets into the detail of what to look out for when buying a used 3 Series BMW. The first is that buyers should always seek out the addresses of local non-franchised BMW specialists. They will be able to assist in keeping an older car in good condition, and their prices are invariably lower than those of the franchised dealerships. Some of them may also offer cars for sale or know of customers who are thinking of selling. And, above all, they are enthusiastic about the marque. In addition, the older the car, the more worthwhile its owner will find joining one of the many enthusiasts' clubs, where like-minded owners can share problems and offer advice based on experience. Contact addresses for these clubs can be found in the classic-car magazines that are published regularly, and in specialist magazines such as Britain's *BMW Car*.

BUYING AN E21 MODEL

The first-generation 3 Series cars were remarkable machines in their day, but they have not worn very well. The later cars to wear 3 Series badges were so much better in so many areas that the early ones quickly fell out of favour. As a result, many also fell on hard times, and good examples are surprisingly uncommon now, a quarter of a century after the first of the E21s took to the roads.

The E21 range also lacked the magic of an M3 flagship to give it an enduring image. In its day, the most exciting factory-built E21 variant was the 323i built between 1978 and 1982. It offered stunning performance for a compact saloon, together with quite affordable running costs. Unfortunately, it also showed up the vices of the E21 range more than any other model. One friend of the author's managed to write off his 323i quite spectacularly when the oversteer for which the car was notorious got the better of him on a wet road.

So, what are the best buys in the E21 range? The Baur hardtop-cabriolet models are still quite desirable, even to those who have no special interest in BMWs, so these are likely to be the most expensive. Otherwise, and broadly speaking, all the six-cylinder cars are preferable to the four-cylinder models. They have better performance, tend to be better equipped, and offer more of the characteristic BMW driving enjoyment. But in view of the rate with which the E21s are now disappearing, no enthusiast should turn his or her nose up at a really well-preserved example of a four-cylinder model.

The bodyshell of the E21 suffers far more from rust than that of later 3 Series models. This is not simply because the cars are that much older; it is because corrosion protection improved on the later designs. E21 models did not have full underseal applied as a matter of course when they were new, for example, and those which have survived tend to be those which were undersealed at an early stage by a fastidious owner.

The more obvious areas where rust breaks out are the rims of the front and rear wheelarches, the front wings in general, the bottoms of the doors, the sills, the rear valance and the metal around the fuel filler neck. Stone chips on the nose and under the bumper also turn into rust eventually, but the damage tends to be cosmetic rather than structural in these areas. Worth remembering, too, is that it is very difficult indeed to blend in new areas of metallic paint on cars which have it; localized repairs really do need to be finished by an expert if they are not to look like localized repairs when the job is finished.

Rust also attacks a number of less easily visible areas, and it is important to poke around carefully when checking over a car for sale. There may be problems lurking in the corners of the floor, around the jacking points, and in the boot floor. All these problems begin as small ones and later turn into major nightmares. So, if an otherwise sound car is showing the first signs of rust in any of these areas, it is advisable to get it cut out as early as possible.

The four-cylinder engines in the E21 cars have a justified reputation for toughness, but most examples will probably now have exceeded the 70,000-mile watershed at which problems begin to arise. Water pump wear is common, but the main problem is top-end noise caused by worn valvetrain components. In particular, the camshaft chain wears, and the cam lobes start to round off at high mileages. None of these problems is prohibitively expensive to fix, but a noisy engine in a four-cylinder E21 offered for sale suggests that the owner has not put much effort into keeping it mechan-

ically sound. There may therefore be other mechanical problems which have been similarly neglected.

Strangely, perhaps, the six-cylinder engines do not have quite such a good reputation. Worth remembering is that the high-performance 323i is likely to have been used hard, and so the engine in such a car may be more worn than that in a 320i of comparable mileage. A number of cars suffered from porous cylinder head castings when they were new, and BMW replaced problem examples under warranty. However, it is possible that there are still some low-mileage engines around which have not yet suffered from the problem. Cylinder heads can also give trouble at high mileages, and the M60 sixes have a reputation for cracking their cylinder heads. Water loss or water mixing with the oil (and vice versa) are the obvious symptoms.

Fuel systems also have their own problems. The original Solex Pierburg carburettors fitted to many engines are next to impossible to put right when they go wrong, so many owners have swapped them for Weber equivalents. In particular, the four-choke Solex 4A1 used on the six-cylinder 320 engine has a bad reputation. As for the fuel injection systems, poor cold starting and poor fuel economy usually mean that some adjustment is needed. Fortunately, as the K-Jetronic injection systems are primarily mechanical, this is not as much of a problem as it sounds. Poor starting in cold weather can also be the result of salt or water on the HT leads.

Gearboxes and axles are durable, and the Getrag five-speed gearbox is a particularly tough component. However, the clutch hydraulics may develop leaks, which are usually first noticed when fluid finds its way onto the pedals and the driver's side carpet. The ZF automatic transmission is also pretty strong, but it can exhibit some strange behaviour if it has been abused. Once the friction bands become damaged, the transmission is essentially fit only for scrap.

The suspension is robust enough, but hard driving wears out the bushes on the front anti-roll bar, which eventually shear. Strangely, stability does not appear to deteriorate when this occurs, but the condition is detectable by increased noise from the front end. Steering is usually trouble-free, but any stickiness needs to be investigated. A common cause is damage to the rack caused by jacking the car here instead of on the cross-member. Right-hand drive cars may suffer from corrosion of the remote linkage to the brake servo (the linkage is direct on left-hand drive examples), and the rear discs of the 323i are likely to corrode if the car is not used regularly.

BUYING AN E30 MODEL

The E30 range offers a tempting array of desirable models, from the M3 and the cabriolets, down through the six-cylinders. There is little demand for diesels or four-cylinder models, except as everyday cars, but they are nonetheless very competent machines which exhibit all the engineering quality of the other E30s.

The bodyshell on these cars does not suffer from rust to anything like the same extent as that on the E21s. BMW took special care to protect the sills and the rear wings behind the wheels from rust, and the deep front spoiler was made of rubberized plastic so that it could not corrode. Rust is actually very rare, even on the earliest E30s, but it is worth checking around the rear wheelarches and for exposed areas of metal on the nose and bonnet caused by stone chipping. Any serious rust in the body of an E30 needs very careful investigation, not least because one cause may be poorly-repaired collision damage.

The doors, especially on two-door models and cabriolets, can begin to sag with age. If there is any sign that they do not fit properly, they should be re-hung before more

The crude fake Motorsport badge on this French-registered turbodiesel E30 does not fool anyone – so why do some owners insist on buying such things?

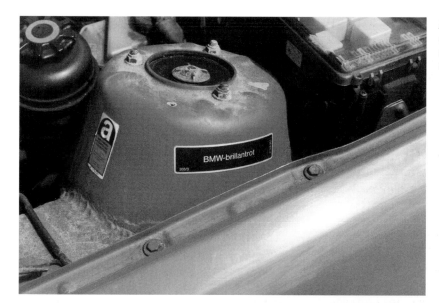

Not sure what colour the car is? All BMWs carry an identifying sticker like this, seen on an E30.

On the more modern BMW engines, many items are concealed behind the plastic covers which are used to improve the underbonnet appearance. This is the engine of an E30 318iS.

serious damage is caused. In most cases, it is advisable to fit new hinges at the same time. The boot sill is high, and so its edges and sealing rubbers are often damaged when loading the boot. Sun-roofs are likely to leak sooner or later, although this prob-

lem is fairly cheap to fix. It is important to check the soft tops of cabriolets, too, because a favourite occupation of low-life characters all over the world is to rip the fabric covering, which is expensive to replace. The soft-top's frame can also rust and, in bad cases, cross-members may be missing. It is quite common to find that some of the hood fasteners have disappeared.

Cracked headlamps can be a bargaining point when buying one of these cars, as their ellipsoidal lamps are more expensive to replace than conventional types. On Touring models, it is the rear lamps which need to be checked carefully, as the bulb-holders inside the car are prone to damage from objects carried in the load area. The E30s built before October 1987 (i.e. the start of the 1988 model-year) have rather more bright metal than later models, and this tends to oxidize. Chrome cleaner applied at the first signs of the problem will prevent it getting worse, and regular applications will keep the problem at bay. In bad cases, however, replacement of the bright parts is the only remedy.

Inside, the E30s are generally hard-wearing, whether equipped with the standard cloth or optional leather upholstery. Worth having are the sports seats, mainly found on the 323i and 325i, which give better support and more adjustment than the standard items. The driver's seat will, of course, be the first one to show signs of wear and tear, and the kick-panels can come adrift from the rear of both the standard front seats. This problem needs to be attended to immediately, otherwise the kick-panels can twist when the seats are used and the seat frames themselves can crack.

The electrical systems on the E30s are generally reliable, although some items can give trouble. Some cars seem prone to one problem after another, while others seem to be relatively free of them. Electric window motors can burn out, and the central locking sometimes fails because of poor connections inside the doors. Also worth knowing is that the Service Interval Indicator on the facia is not infallible. It operates from Ni-Cad batteries which lose their charge after five or six years and cause the indicator lights to give confusing readings. At the same time, the rev counter may fail intermittently, and the temperature gauge may fluctuate. Simply replacing the batteries rarely cures the problem and, as often as not, the circuit board itself has to be changed as well. Note that early types with three LEDs cost more than the later types which have just one.

The four-cylinder engines should be good for 150,000 miles without major overhaul. They have chain-driven camshafts, and the chains can wear and become slack. A distinctive chain rattle at idle gives this condition away. Listen particularly for top-end rattle on the four-valve engines, which have more componentry to make more noise! The six-cylinder engines can run up to 200,000 miles, unless failure of the cam-belt necessitates a major rebuild before that. When buying, it is important to discover how long ago the cam-belt was changed, as belts can fray and snap without warning after they have reached a certain mileage. Worth knowing is that the 323i engine seems to have disappointing low-speed torque, even when perfectly healthy.

The electronic fuel injection systems on most of these cars give little trouble, unless water has got into the petrol. If it has done so in quantity, it can set up rusting inside the precision-engineered elements of the injection system. This leads to problems such as poor starting and misfiring, and replacement of all the affected components is likely to prove expensive. The electronically-controlled carburettors on the early 316 can be troublesome. They rely on an air-fuel sensor, which sometimes fails to transmit its readings correctly to the carburettor. This leads to poor performance and poor economy, and repairs are time-consuming and expensive. The US-model 318i is also notorious for bogging-down during hard acceleration from rest.

Buying an E30 M3

The E30 M3 remains one of the most desirable of all BMWs, and for that reason some cars which are well past their best have been hastily fettled to look good. Make no mistake: a rough example of an M3 will quickly become a running sore in its owner's wallet. This is why it is vitally important to check very thoroughly indeed the condition and history of any car offered for sale. It would be unnecessarily restrictive to advise against buying a car with no service history, if only because the M3 is so desirable. However, buyers of such cars should enter the deal with their eyes wide open. The best bet when buying an M3 is always to go for an unmolested example which has been properly maintained.

The only external panel on an M3 which is the same as that on an ordinary E30 is the bonnet. There are so few M3s around that few specialists will keep replacement panels in stock, so delays are to be expected in sourcing major parts. Pattern front wings, in both steel and GRP, have been available. Worth knowing is that when new, the cars had a line of body-colour seam-sealing compound where the top rear corner of each wing meets the windscreen surround. If it is not there, the wing has been taken off, and it is worth finding out why this was done. There is a very good chance that the wing was removed and replaced after collision damage. If so, a further careful examination is going to be very necessary: the car could have been in a nasty high-speed smash. Poor repair work will reduce the value of an M3, and might even reduce its safety at speed, too. Uneven panel gaps, rippled wings and bumpers or chin spoilers that do not fit neatly are all signs that a car may have been rebuilt after an accident.

Regular oil and filter changes are vital on the M3 engine. Oil leaks may be found at the head gasket, at the front crankshaft seal in the timing cover, at the sump gasket and around the oil-pressure relief valve on the oil filter housing. They are best attended to as soon as possible. Some valvetrain noise from the engine is normal, but excessive noise from the timing chain means a replacement is necessary. This is not cheap. The four-valve motor should also idle smoothly. If not, the cause might be leaks in the flexible rubbers between cylinder head and manifold; unfortunately, it might equally well be bent valves caused by over-revving. Also worth noting is that the alternator mounting bushes can deteriorate with time, allowing the alternator to move out of true and giving rise to rapid fan belt wear, poor charging and a host of other minor maladies.

Small oil leaks from the gearbox and final drive are acceptable. There may well be wear in the mountings of the final drive and this will, of course, be exacerbated by hard use. There are bushes at each end of the transverse sub-frame which carries the final drive, and when these wear the sub-frame moves under acceleration to give a disconcerting amount of rear-wheel steering. The final drive itself has a large rubber mounting, and this must be intact.

Finally, the top and bottom steering ball-joints are susceptible to wear, and slack in the steering rack will indicate worn inner knuckle joints.

Cylinder head overhauls on these engines are expensive, and work on the heads of the six-cylinder cars obviously tends to be more expensive than its equivalent on four-cylinder types, M3s excepted. All cylinder heads can crack, usually directly below the camshaft and between its bearing journals. In engines which have not been run for some time, the oil seals in the valve-guides harden. This allows oil to be drawn down the bores and to appear as smoke in the exhaust, which will lead to failure of the emissions test carried out annually in many countries. Oil leaks, however, need not be so serious: it is worth checking the gasket sealing the camshaft cover before assuming the worst.

Overheating may be caused by cylinder head corrosion. Unless anti-freeze is used in the cooling system all year round, the waterways in the alloy cylinder head can corrode. Small pieces of corroded alloy then break away and circulate round the cooling system, eventually causing partial blockage of the waterways or the radiator. Cooling problems may also be caused by a failure of the heat-sensitive viscous coupling on the engine fan.

Exhausts can give trouble, too. The nuts securing the manifold work loose, and the exhaust starts to blow. Unless great care is taken – and sometimes even then – the studs can shear when the nuts are re-tight-

ened. This is an expensive problem to rectify, because the only way to do the job properly is to remove the cylinder head and drill out the broken studs. The manifold itself could crack on early 325i engines, but most will now have been replaced by the improved later design.

Both manual and automatic gearboxes are robust and dependable units, and are unlikely to give major trouble. The intermediate gears tend to whine in the manual boxes, for some reason especially so in the four-cylinder models. Manual gearchanges

Practicality can be an important decision in influencing the choice of a 3 Series. The hatchback E36 Compact models offer loadspace versatility . . .

. . . while there is even more room in the back of an E36 Touring. However, the Touring models do not have the load capacity of some competitive estates.

eventually become rather sloppy, which is usually the result of worn linkages. The bearings of a high-mileage manual gearbox may also rattle at idle when the gearbox is hot, but this is irritating more than anything else. The noise actually sounds worse than it is, because it is amplified by the gearbox's alloy casing. Clutches can last for 100,000 miles with care, and are no more costly or difficult to replace than on any ordinary car.

Suspension components are tough, but the front wishbone ball joints can wear. In such cases, the cure involves replacing the entire wishbone assembly. All E30s feel rather nose-heavy when cornering, but the optional sports suspension goes some way towards correcting this and is worth having. The front struts can wear more quickly on a hard-driven car, and the result is a sloppy feeling about the front end. Rear tyres tend to wear rather more quickly than those at the front, partly because of the semi-trailing arms' geometry, and partly because enthusiastic drivers tend to scrub off the rubber in hard cornering! Many cars have had their suspension lowered (mainly for effect rather than in any real bid to improve handling or road-holding), and it is vital to check how this has been done before buying a modified example. If the wrong dampers were used with the modified suspension, the rear wheels could hit the inner wings and cause them to crack.

BUYING AN E36 MODEL

The E36 range offers an even wider variety of models than its predecessors. Most desirable, as before, are the M3 and convertible types, but the two-door coupés are also very attractive propositions. The four-door saloon has disappointing rear legroom (BMW still had not got the interior propor-

As alloy wheels became more popular, so BMW designed plastic wheel trims for their cheaper models which looked like cast alloy wheels. This style was introduced on the 1997 E36 models, and was certainly quite convincing on first glance. Plastic wheel trims can suffer from kerbing damage, just as alloy wheels can.

tions right) but is otherwise very practical, and the Touring estate is a useful everyday holdall with a dash of style thrown in for good measure. Compacts have their devotees and detractors; they are, at least, generally more affordable than many of the other models.

Rust is something which has not yet affected the bodyshells of the E36 cars, even though the oldest examples have now been on the road for ten years. As with the E30 models, therefore, any rust in the structure should be treated with the gravest suspicion. The most likely cause is a poorly-executed repair, and evidence of such treatment should lead the E36 buyer to two conclusions. First is that the car has been involved in an accident at some time. Second is that at least one of the car's owners was not

Electronic distance recorders make it difficult for the seller of a modern BMW to falsify the distance readout. This one is seen on a German-market 323ti Compact. However, you should always try to verify that the mileage shown on the car is genuine – the 3 Series cars generally wear so well that it is difficult to estimate from a casual inspection how many miles one has covered.

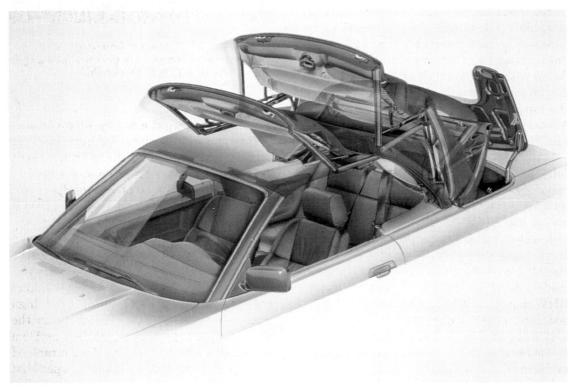

The convertibles are attractive purchases, but do check the condition of the soft top. The fabric is often vandalized and cannot be repaired satisfactorily, so the only solution is a complete new covering – which is expensive. Check that the mechanism works properly, too, and that there is no rust in the framework. Shown is an E36 model.

prepared to spend the money to keep it in first-class condition. The implications of both are obvious.

Interior items wear well. Quality control was actually quite a big problem in the early days of the E36, but most cars were sorted out under warranty. The problems were in any case niggling: window winders fell off, glove-boxes fell open, and door trims worked loose. Electric windows can fail, especially the most frequently-used one on the driver's side, and shuddering of the glass as it rises or falls gives warning of imminent failure. Fortunately, the E36 does not have the problems with its Service Interval Indicator boards which plagued the earlier E30 models.

The E36 models were certainly built to last, and all models can reasonably be expected to rack up mileages of 250,000 or more as long as they are serviced in accordance with their maker's recommendations. The M40 four-cylinder engines do not have the top end weaknesses of the earlier fours, although they can suffer from premature camshaft wear.

Six-cylinder weaknesses are also mercifully few. Water pumps seem to fail surprisingly often, and sometimes there are ignition problems caused by the failure of one or more of the individual cylinder ignition coils. There was considerable publicity in the mid-1990s when some examples of the M52 engine in the 320i, 323i and 328i models developed premature bore wear, but BMW moved swiftly to contain the problem and later engines were modified. However, it is still possible that some early examples of these engines may eventually develop problems.

Both four-cylinder and six-cylinder engines have hydraulic self-adjusting tappets, which begin to wear after around 90,000 miles. Top end rattle is the result, but the problem is not a major one if it is

The modern BMW depends heavily on sophisticated electronics; components such as these, from an E36 M3, are not DIY propositions.

attended to straight away by simply changing the tappets. All cars also have catalytic converters in their exhausts, with the result that replacement of an exhaust system is a major expense. It is advisable to check, when buying an E36, how long the exhaust system has been on the car!

The ZF automatic gearboxes are long-lived and generally trouble-free. The manual types may suffer from obstructive synchromesh on second gear when cold, and they can growl a little after very high mileages. Clutch judder, especially on the four-cylinder models, is a notorious problem for which there seems to be no guaranteed cure. In some cases, however, specialist attention does do the trick.

Suspension problems are limited. The lower front ball joints can wear, but these can be quickly and easily replaced. Rear damper top mountings can also wear out quite quickly, and this problem is revealed by a rattle from the back of the car as it passes over rough surfaces. Handling, ride and road-holding are all superb, but enthusiasts argue that the E30-derived rear suspension of the Compact models denies them the handling balance and finesse of the other E36 models.

BUYING AN E46 MODEL

As this book goes to press, the E46 models have been available for just over a year. Build quality is second to none once again, and no major problems have yet shown up. It is probable that the cars will go on to have an even better service record than the enviable one of their E36 predecessors.

However, it will be worth remembering in a few years' time, as these cars pass on to their third and fourth owners, that their complex electronic and other systems are not a DIY proposition. Buyers of older E46s are bound to become reliant on specialist garages, whether holding a BMW franchise or not. This should mean that more cars will be maintained to the manufacturer's standards, but it is also likely to mean that corners will be cut wherever possible in an effort to save money. A well-worn E46 which has not been properly serviced is probably not going to be a good buy in the second decade of the 21st century.

Index

Index